Nigel

Nigel

my family and other dogs

MONTY DON

www.tworoadsbooks.com

First published in Great Britain in 2016 by Two Roads
An imprint of John Murray Press
An Hachette UK company

First published in paperback in 2017

18

A CIP catalogue record for this title is available from the British Library

Paperback ISBN 978 1 473 64171 6
Ebook ISBN 978 1 473 64172 3
Audio Digital Download ISBN 978 1 473 64820 3

Typeset by Palimpsest Book Production Ltd, Falkirk, Stirlingshire

Printed and bound by Clays Ltd, Elcograf S.p.A.

Hodder & Stoughton policy is to use papers that are natural, renewable and recyclable products and made from wood grown in sustainable forests. The logging and manufacturing processes are expected to conform to the environmental regulations of the country of origin.

Hodder & Stoughton Ltd
Carmelite House
50 Victoria Embankment
London EC4Y 0DZ

www.hodder.co.uk

For Adam Don – a true master

'The more I see of men,
the more I admire dogs'
Madame de Staël

Contents

Nigel

Introduction

My father had a golden retriever called Barney that he adored. In fact he never came home with us when, as a family, we returned from his posting in Germany in 1956 when I was aged one, so I have no memory of Barney at all. I only knew him from the photograph that my father kept on his desk to the day he died, nearly 30 years ago.

From the little black and white print I have of my father and Barney, Barney looks very like Nell, my new golden retriever puppy. My father, pipe in hand, is clearly posing, while Barney has turned away as the shutter was pressed. On the back, in my mother's handwriting it says, 'This is a grand one of you both isn't it? April 24th, 1948'. Even though it was to be another seven years before I was born and I never knew Barney, the picture is redolent of nostalgia. It is a lost world.

My father is still only 32 and yet, after six years of war, looks older; completely devoid of any of the boyishness that today's middle-aged men cling to. Although he's pictured in a double-breasted suit, he was a career soldier, a champion boxer, wartime commando, who never found his place in civilian life, never found much ease in life at all, save when working or walking outside alone. Yet he loved his dogs with a silent intensity.

I have inherited much from him, not least his black depressions and a certain physical robustness, but also a deep and abiding love of dogs. I grew up with dogs and, from the age of 21 when I was given my own dog for the first time, I have never been without at least one.

For me a garden without my dogs would be as empty as a garden without plants. For the 25 years that I have been in this garden, I can honestly say that I have always had at least one dog within a few yards of me. It is their garden as much as mine. Chewed bits of stick are strategically deposited around the place. At any one time at least half a dozen used yellow tennis balls are dotted under the hedges and in the borders. Every morning, first thing, Nigel and I walk round together, sniffing the air, opening the chickens and working the day out. Last thing at night we repeat the walk by torchlight although, as this is followed by a biscuit, there is a slightly more excited tone to the proceedings.

But there is nothing unusual in this. Perhaps most of us would willingly share our lives with a dog. Each one is special and each one individual, but the love is uncomplicated and common to all of us.

But right from the beginning, Nigel has been different. It helps that he is good looking – beautiful even – but so are lots of dogs and, anyway, as we do our children, we all think our dogs are fine creatures. But Nigel has that very rare quality of drawing attention to him as if by osmosis. He steals every scene he is in. He takes the light from a room and casts it so that it falls on him to his very best advantage. When we are filming it is uncanny how he will always find just the one position where the combination of sunlight, flowers, the whole composition of the scene – about which he cannot possibly have the slightest notion – all come together to work perfectly around him.

The nearest comparison to Nigel I can make in human terms is President Bill Clinton, with whom I had one brief brush.

Sarah and I were invited to hear him speak at the Hay Literary Festival, and then attend a dinner with him and other guests, who turned out to be every newspaper editor and senior writer and all the most famous authors in the UK at the time.

It was as prestigious a literary audience as this country could put together. Clinton's lecture was actually pretty uninspired and without any of the insights or revelations that I had hoped freedom from office would liberate him to share. He was very late (I later found out that he was practising his golf swing on a friend's lawn) and security meant that all 400 of us were not allowed to leave the tent. There were about a dozen square-shouldered secret service people with ear pieces and dark glasses facing the audience who were getting very restless.

Then Clinton appeared to polite applause . . . and said nothing. For what seemed an agonising length of time, in fact about ten seconds, he looked down, shuffled, looked up, and did and said nothing. At that point the entire audience visibly and audibly leant forward. He had the entire audience craning towards him. He waited a moment or two longer and then started speaking quite softly. By then we were all in the palm of his hand and had all walked gratefully into it.

At the dinner I watched him: every woman was bewitched by him. He was middle-aged, overweight, and yet cast an irresistible spell. But he did not do it by reaching out and obviously charming people. It was as though he was a magnet and, once inside his orbit, they could not resist his pull. Some of this can be put down to the aphrodisiac of power, but he had more charisma – the 'compelling attractiveness' – than anyone else I have come across.

Other than Nigel. Nigel can match anybody for his ability to inspire affection. It does not quite rate as macho a skill as running the world's greatest superpower, but probably does as much good and, anyway, I challenge any politician anywhere to match Nigel at chasing yellow tennis balls. I rest my case.

Nigel inspires real love. Somehow he has been blessed with a rare something that actively improves the lives of those around him – even remotely via television. When he had a terrible accident and broke his back some years ago we received literally sackfuls of letters, most simply addressed to 'Nigel, Longmeadow, Herefordshire'. Every week there are parcels and presents that are delivered, again addressed directly to him. At Christmas he receives more cards than we do. Whenever I give a talk or do a book signing, there will be people who queue patiently simply to hand me a wrapped present to take home for Nigel. If I am filling the car with fuel or buying a newspaper, someone will always tell me that they love my dog or ask how Nigel is.

For a long time I could not quite understand it. What was it that he had that was so special or indeed different from any other dog?

But finally I worked it out. We all love the way that our pet dogs show us unbiased, non-judgemental affection. When we are fed up, distressed, grumpy, or even have behaved badly and done something we know to be wrong, our dogs still love us. But Nigel has the rare gift of taking our love and making us feel enriched and enlarged by doing so. It is not what he gives back to us so much as what he allows us to give to him. The wrapped dog biscuits and soft toys that are sent to him or handed to me in trust to pass on to him are more than just treats. They are symbols of the love that he has empowered us to feel. And, as I saw that evening in Hay-on-Wye, that is a powerful gift to have.

So this is Nigel's story, set in Nigel's garden, which I share with and look after for him. It is also an unashamed celebration of the love I have shared for other dogs in my life and the pleasure and happiness that they have given me.

1. In the Beginning

There was one puppy that caught our eye. Sitting apart from the others, it was barking and had a slightly goofy smile, more Lenny the lion than leonine.

It was 1 July 2008 and my son and I were in the middle of the Forest of Dean. The cottage was set deep in the woods in a clearing down a bumpy grass track. We had the unease of not being sure if this could possibly be the right place, combined with worrying that it was – with all its slightly unnerving remoteness in this, one of the most cut-off bits of the UK – indeed the right place.

Once we were inside it was clear that the whole house was

given over to the cult of the golden retriever. Three or four adult dogs greeted us in the hall, and the kitchen was almost entirely occupied by a mother and her litter of pups.

Outside in the garden were kennels with another, older litter, and two of the most handsome dogs I had ever seen, one with a russet coat, the colour of oak. This was the sire of the pups in the kitchen and a champion obedience triallist. The mother came from a long line of either champion gun dogs or guide dogs for the blind. In other words, these pups were born to be both Good and Beautiful.

But for the moment all these noble virtues lay suppressed beneath a thick layer of cuteness. Few can be immune to the overwhelming charm of a seven-week-old retriever puppy. However, I was sternly practical, smoothing away the wrinkles of sentiment with firm hands.

'Look at them carefully,' I said to my son, 'check the line of their backs, how they hold their heads. We must make sure they have a good hip score. Are they responding with curiosity or fear? We want a dog that is bold and confident. Resist any temptation to rescue the smallest or most timid.'

But I knew this was bluster. Both of us were irresistibly drawn to one that hung a little back and barked most while looking directly into our eyes. The bark was neither hostile nor afraid – simply talkative. This was Nigel.

He hasn't changed at all. He still likes to talk to you and his initial greeting is always a short welcoming bark followed by a deep conversational groaning.

So we chose him, paid our deposit and drove home, wondering what to call him. There had been some discussion already and certain names had strong lobbies within the household.

One school thought that anything remotely pet-like was capitulation to the forces of bourgeois degeneration. So Bracken, Rusty, Max, Captain, Jake or Barney were definitely out. They fought hard for the least suitable name one could think of. The game was made more complex in that it could not be a ridiculous made-up name. It just had to be as inappropriate as possible. Keith was favourite, followed closely by Nigel, with Norman having its fans.

The other lobby – the older, duller and slightly less excitable section, i.e. me – wanted to walk a middle way. It had to sound reasonable when called out in a park or as the dog went about its intended retrieval work in front of other owners and their highly trained dogs. Ted and Tom worked well by this measure. In the end a compromise was struck. Keith, although tempting for its extreme undogginess, was jettisoned in favour of Nigel. His full name would be Nigel Bear, but first-name terms would be adopted by all, although those that know him very well often call him Mr Bear.

So a week after our first visit we drove back to the middle of the Forest and collected Nigel Bear, who, of course, was promptly sick in the car.

2. Nigel is Introduced to His Garden

On that first day I took Nigel round the garden in my arms, showing him what we had made and what we would share. You lay your offerings down, reveal yourself.

I have shown this garden to scores of people, knowing from the first minute that they perhaps admired but did not understand at all. This is not in the least offensive – nothing is worse than the burden of having to pay sufficient dues to someone's garden while they watch with beady eyes to make sure that you are being congratulatory enough. In any event I always find showing people round tricky, because this garden – any garden – is loaded with so much more than the surface floral display that might be there at any one time or in any season. The whole point of gardens is that they accrue, with all the weight of love and time and care that you might spend on making a long-lasting and deep human relationship. There are good days and bad days, but the strength of the relationship endures.

But you do not demand any approval or acclaim from your dogs. The whole point was to show Nigel our garden – not what I had done. This was his new kingdom.

Nigel quickly learned that putting on my boots was a call to arms that would rouse him from the deepest slumber, and that whereas the front door means the car, visitors, perhaps even strangers to bark at, the back door means the garden and the fields beyond and is only ever occupied by friends and willing ball-throwers. As soon as I open it he charges out, tail held high, shooting into the greenhouse yard to see if there is anyone there he can greet.

The garden is where we set off to every day. It is our outside. When I lived with my dogs in London, the garden was a place for them to lie outside but not a place to go. One of the many good things about living in the country is that you have much more space. The cost of a modest London flat will buy you rolling acres. So our morning walk round the garden involves throwing balls, chasing rabbits, feeding the chickens, sniffing out a thousand tantalising smells, as well as a gate at the end of the garden opening directly on to fields, where we can walk for miles before coming to any kind of road. It is doggy (and human) heaven.

But in the beginning everything was new, strange and a little alarming. For the first few days we hardly ventured beyond the greenhouse or Cottage Garden, and then gradually extended our forays until we reached the orchard at the far end. The garden is not that huge – barely two acres – but for an eight-week-old puppy it was uncharted territory, where in all likelihood 'there be dragons' lurking round every hedge and corner.

After a few weeks he became brave enough to be left outside for ten minutes or so at a time (whereas for the first few days if he disappeared even for a few minutes the refrain was 'Where's puppy?' fearing he was either in or causing trouble). I remember one very sweet moment when he was about twelve weeks old when I had gone outside without him, leaving the back door open. Suddenly I saw this little body run between the hedges in the Cottage Garden, stop, run back, charge round the corner and rush up to me, ears pressed anxiously back, delighted and relieved to find me. It meant that he was starting to know his way around – and also wanted to locate me, which, of course, flatters and melts any dog-loving heart. We were becoming a team.

~

One of my favourite pictures of Nigel is taken when he had been with us just a few days. He had tentatively ventured outside, going from the house into the Lime Walk. He moved slowly and carefully, sniffing this strange world – probably outside on his own for the first time ever. When he reached the turning to the box balls (as yet untouched by blight), he started to veer left, when something must have caught his attention; the camera has fixed that second when the back half of his body is still turning left while the front is going the opposite direction, so that his two front legs are completely crossed – and the next second he fell over in an undignified heap.

His joints collapse both predictably and seemingly entirely at random, so he flops and rolls and subsides with almost every movement – yet is completely acrobatic and flexible, so simply converts the collapse into the next movement, which might well collapse on him too. This capacity for extreme contortion followed by collapse has never left him.

Nigel quickly learned the map of this new world and made it his own.

So this is Nigel's garden, the centre of his world, and mine.

3. Puppy

All puppies are sweet. That is their default position. But no puppy was ever sweeter than Nigel. It was not just that he was a cuddly ball of golden fur with a fat tummy, overlarge auburn ears and a shining charcoal nose – all pretty much guaranteed to melt the least mushy heart – but that he radiated a kind of existential innocence based upon a combination of absolute trust and limited brainpower.

This little puppy, predictably cute and innocent, also had a distinct air of decency. From the very first, Nigel has always been a good egg.

I have been looking back at pictures that I took on the day

we went to get him, 8 July 2008, and it is very striking that the mature dog is right there from the first. In many ways he arrived fully formed. The fact that he could be held in one hand simply meant that he was just waiting to grow into himself.

Far from being just an identikit puppy, everything about him – the way he moved, held himself, flopped, huffed his breath, pretended to be a growly bear, watched obsessively for a favoured ball, and even the way he tolerated being cuddled, as though all we adult humans were slightly over-whelming maiden aunts pressing their affection on a birthday visit – are all still there in the adult dog.

For the first few moments after our arrival at Longmeadow, he buried himself into my armpit, clearly completely over-whelmed after being separated for the first time from the rest of the litter, a three-hour journey and introduction to a house-hold of five strange dogs, all barking and suspicious. He smelt of sawdust, biscuits and, rather regrettably, of sick.

He was ridiculously, rather unbelievably, soft. His fur was like the best cashmere and his body almost muscle free – barely able to carry his own weight, so he would skid and flop as he moved, surprised by the load on his legs.

I had prepared myself for this and expected a slow unfurling over a matter of days. In fact it took minutes. After the briefest of retreats he poked his head up, had a good look around and clamoured to get down. From that moment he was interested in everything. Everything was new and entertaining. Grass was odd but had real possibilities of being plucked like a chicken. Pots of plants managed to be both hard and soft – and the soft bits could be pulled, which, if you hit the sweet spot, resulted in the whole shebang being pulled over and the hard bit breaking. Bull's-eye.

But first we had to get to know each other. I remember the overwhelming feeling I had when my first child was born was that I did not know him. He was a complete stranger who I fell in love with at first sight. And so the complicated relationship of father and son begins. If less intense, it is just like that with a new dog. The slow but headlong plunge into lasting love begins.

What makes it so especially rewarding is that the dog learns every bit as much about you as you do them. They read your body language infinitely more subtly than you read theirs and relate with exquisite sensitivity to the rhythms of your day.

Everything interested him. But his attention span was somewhere between three and ten seconds. Mostly at the three end. This made life a series of distractions and diversions.

For the first few days he could not see above knee level. When you bent down it was an arrival – a surprise visit. But after a week he was looking up and seeing more and starting to recognise our outlines.

Nigel has always been noisy, quick to voice his demands and emotions with a range of sounds that soon became recognisable. When he wanted attention or was frustrated he produced a surprisingly deep, rolling, wuh wuh wuh. But when locked in and wanting to get out, usually because there was a suspicion of food the other side of the closed door, then he had an indignant high-pitched yelp.

But he never once cried or barked at night, even on the first night, which was the very first time he had been on his own – and in a strange place to boot. We wound him down with lots of sleepy suggestive noises and cuddles before putting him to bed in the back kitchen with a soft toy for company. We tiptoed round, breath bated, waiting for the howls and cries. They never came. I now know what was going on in his mind. It was bedtime. So he went to bed and went to sleep. That's what a chap does.

4. The Front

M ost houses have a front garden of sorts and most front gardens are the transition between public and private spaces. The outside world looks in and yet enters only by invitation or on business. You can do what you like with it but everything is open to public scrutiny. Front gardens are looked at from the outside so the house is their backdrop, whereas back gardens are mostly viewed from the house.

However, the front garden at Longmeadow is hidden from the public gaze and always has been. One of the first things we did when we started to make the garden was to section off an area of the front lawn furthest from the house and plant a hedge to screen it from the house, and to screen the garden from the road. It is where the children always used to play when they were little because, despite making what I thought were much better and more interesting places for them to play elsewhere, small children will always play close to the house and run in and out as much as possible. In this, as in lots of other ways, the Front (somehow it has never been called the front garden) is as much house as garden, and so fulfils the traditional role of the front garden as the link between the house and outer world.

This is where Nigel lies in the sun, benevolent gatekeeper and observer, watching the world go by. Not that there is much traffic, mechanical or human. Cars come down the lane perhaps once or twice an hour and the click of the front gate nearly always means it is a member of the family to be greeted with a wagging tail and shouty barking rather than a stranger heralded by a tail held stiffly upright and the bark edged with hostility. Nigel, like most dogs, seems to have an uncanny sense of which car is which; when one of ours is approaching, he shows signs of excitement before my ears can pick up any sound at all.

It is a very simple space, dominated by clipped yew cones set in grass and bounded by yew hedges. I bought about a third of the yews from a tree auction in 1993, although they were a fraction of the size they are now, and the outer line was planted about five years later, using spare hedging plants that have gradually become solid and imposing through years of clipping. Only the stone of the path that runs from the front gate to the front door breaks the shades of green layering on green. It makes a symmetrical formal entry to the house and is very easy to maintain. The grass is mown every ten days or so and the yew clipped once a year in late August or early September. That is it. It is a garden that barely needs any gardening.

The yew cones also make the perfect place to play hide and seek for both children and puppies, and Nigel when young would whirl around and between them in figures of eight, ears back, his scamper slightly hysterical, like an over-excited child. When Nell appeared she woke in him that playful spirit again, and the two of them often race dizzyingly among them.

In fact this path continues, without changing or breaking its step in any way, through the house and on out through the back door to the Spring Garden. Everything that has to be brought from a car to the house, be it food, shopping, or luggage, is ferried in a wheelbarrow straight into the kitchen – with Nigel trotting alongside trying to deposit a ball into the barrow before it stops.

For the first five years that we were at Longmeadow,

everything that had to get to the other side of the garden – which is almost all the garden – had to make its way down this path and through the front door, into the hall, through the back kitchen and out of the back door to become garden-worthy. This included not just all the plants, thousands of fencing rods and stakes, manure and compost, but also the chickens and Charlie the cantankerous Shetland pony. Perhaps this entrance to their new world imprinted itself on to them, because we always left our garden doors wide open if it is vaguely warm, and Charlie and the hens would wander into the kitchen in search of something to nibble.

Charlie is long gone and the foxes and mink have eaten generations of chickens since those first introductions, but our doors are still left open from early morning until night and the swallows and martins swoop in and out of the house, sweeping down the entrance hall and round the corner into the barn-like open Tudor hall. They usually do a turn or two and then scythe out as they came, but occasionally a young one will become confused and spend a day or two in the house, sleeping on the beams before eventually making its way back outside. And in winter it is not uncommon to see a movement from the corner of one's eye and be joined as you sit by the fire by the mouse-like darts of a little wren that has slipped through an open door into the warmth of the house.

5. Morning Smells

The day begins with song. The light is implied, guessed at, just a slight eastern glimmer behind the clouds.

Through this breaks the first tentative call of a robin. Clear, fluting and brave. For a few minutes he holds the stage and then, gradually, as though from a distance, a thousand birds begin to mark the day. Blackbird battles blackbird and the thrush stakes its claim from the top of its favourite plum tree. Behind the melodies is a counterpoint of peeps and tweets and cheeps and three-note trills.

However tired I am, I cannot resist either the dawn chorus or the first light. The day calls. I slip out of bed, go straight to the window – facing east and always open, always curtain-less – and look across the fields to get a sense of the weather.

Then I throw on some clothes and tiptoe downstairs, trying not to wake the rest of the household, but this stealth (admit-tedly not my strongest point) is invariably made irrelevant by a short bark from Nigel. Perhaps he hears the slight creak of the stairs, or more probably he can smell me as clearly as I can hear the birdsong. Either way, this slightly muffled, slightly overpitched and overexcited sound is his standard greeting.

This morning bark seems to surprise him as much as anything else, as he is pulled from a much deeper sleep than my own. He scrambles to his feet and is fully awake by the time he is upright, rushing past me straight to the front door where he stands too close, tail vertical and wagging. Then, as there has been every day for the past six years, the half-shuffle, half-dance into reverse as, against all expectations, the door pulls a fast one and opens inwards on him, as it has done and will do every time. But with that he is outside, head up, taking deep draughts of morning air.

We can only guess at the layers of sophistication on offer to a dog's nose. But we do know that the finest *parfumeur*, blessed (or perhaps cursed) with hyperosmia, is the bluntest of instruments compared to the most casual canine snuffle. Humans apparently have six million olfactory cells making up our two million scent receptors, which pales into insignificance behind a dog's 220 million. Our own ability to detect scent is astonishingly subtle – we are equipped to detect some odours in dilutions of one part to over a billion parts of air – but that only highlights how precise and unimaginably refined a dog's nose must be.

We know that dogs' brains work with smell in the same way that ours do, insomuch as that, like us, their scent receptors send their messages to the most primitive part of the brain that also deals with emotion. In other words, what a dog smells has as much influence on how it feels as anything else, and almost certainly more powerfully so. We have all experienced the pang of memory that comes as you break the skin of an orange, unscrew a jar of jam, or lean forward and suddenly catch the faintest breath of a perfume last smelt at the nape of your mother's neck when you were a toddler. A thousand smells pull a thousand triggers, without any perceptible thought process or rationalisation. The response is visceral, emotional and even spiritual. Imagine how it must be for dogs, then, with all these responses multiplied ten thousand times. It also means that association through smell is a powerful tool for training. An article of clothing will be comforting for a dog, not because it feels nice or looks like their owners or reminds them of happy times, but because it smells of happiness and security. Putting your hand in your pocket will trigger the response of the dog sitting expectantly waiting for the titbit that sometimes follows that action, not just because it has learnt that particular body-action, but also because the scent of the morsel of biscuit has left a memory that is as powerfully pleasing as the original delicious flood of biscuity smell. Their memory of scent is as emotional as ours – only fine-tuned to a degree beyond our ken. Compared to our own noses, which clutch at scent and struggle to articulate it in any coherent language, it seems as though dogs read smells with the fluency of a professional translator – only one that has worked in a thousand languages simultaneously.

Along with almost every dog I know, Nigel is addicted to yellow tennis balls. If we buy a new batch he can smell them inside their casing inside a shopping basket and becomes frantic with excitement. I suspect that there must be something in the yellow dye that dogs particularly love, because for the first half-hour or so he bites and drops and picks up the ball repeatedly, stimulating and releasing that swoony scent. Then, once this initial delirium has worn off, he will rank the accumulating tennis balls in order of preference; if I take three or four in my pockets when we go for a walk, he will clearly differentiate between them, even though to my eye they look identical and are often caked in mud and worse.

My own sense of smell is not particularly good by human standards, and the only way that I can imagine what Nigel must be absorbing is to think of his nose absorbing information in the same way that I lie in bed listening to the dawn chorus, with its receding layers of sound, each bound into all the sights and knowledge of the bird that made it, so that the whole comes together as a kind of three-dimensional tapestry, bound tight to make a coherent picture, but with every stitch clear and separate and minutely observable.

So Nigel stands for a moment, lost in the richness of mist, damp leaves, worm-tilled earth, cobwebs on the yew, a ripe tang from pear, apple, shrivelled damson and hawthorn, each with their own folds of fruity complexities, bird feather and hint of vole, the thrilling trace of rabbit from the field and a delicious touch of biscuit crumbled two days ago from a careless hand. There is the leather of my boots mixed with the rubber, mud and sheepy smear from my son's wellies, the slightly fungal trace from the log I dropped from the barrowload I brought in yesterday, and the milkman's trousers the other side of the gate, gone these thirty minutes but still leaving a hint of the last dozen houses he has visited.

Occasionally Nigel's nose becomes obsessed with one scent to the exclusion of all others. It is as though one particular smell so dominates all others that nothing else can be considered. Almost always this is made confusing because no human nose (well, not mine at least) can perceive anything at all. The most obvious example is a bitch on heat half a mile away, which will reduce Nigel and any male dog to a gibbering, sex-crazed wreck. But often I never discover what is dominating his airwaves to such an extent. I remember when he was about six months old he went through a phase of being fascinated by the grass between our topiary yew cones in front of the house. No square inch was unworthy of intense inspection, his nose pressed against the grass, blowing and sucking like a questing pig. I would vainly call him but he was lost in whatever fragrant and fascinating worlds he found there. Then he would suddenly look up as though from a dream, his ears drop in what looked like apology and bound over as if to say, 'So sorry, lost myself for a moment there, what was it you were saying?'

Now the adult, worldly Nigel reads the morning air like a saloon-bar gent scanning his daily paper. He flicks his nostrils left to right and back again, finds it all good, has a detailed inspection of the corner of the clipped yew where every dog for the past twenty years has left his mark, a ritual cock of the leg and the brisk march back inside.

He ignores the open door to his own bed in the back kitchen and strides to the fake-fur-lined wooden box next to the Aga, and gently but firmly crams himself into it. It is far too small. He can fit in his body and three legs in one go, but has to substitute another limb if he wants to curl his head inside. It looks excruciatingly uncomfortable but he loves it.

That is enough excitement for the next hour or so, and while I take my cup of tea to my desk, Nigel huffs a long sigh and sinks back down into sleep in the lovely warm awkwardness of the kitchen bed.

6. First Dogs, Early Days

I grew up in a tiny village in north Hampshire, in a house my great-grandfather had built a hundred years before I was born. The immediate area around the village was rich with a tangle of hedges, small fields, slithers of spinneys and great blocks of beech woods and hazel coppices. The spinneys and woods were carpeted with primroses and violets at Easter, followed by bluebells in May. These woods were more of an influence on me than any garden, and the combination of their dappled light, drifts of small but sturdy flowers and the managed coppice woods with great standard trees has been the model for my idealised landscape and garden ever since.

So I built camps and played in the woods as much as I possibly could, free from constraint or rules and connected to home by the large gong that hung in the hall; my mother would stand on the front door steps, whacking it with its round leather hammer so the sound pealed around the village, bringing us running across the fields.

I can clearly remember slipping out of bed at six a.m. on a bright summer's morning, pulling on a T-shirt and shorts and my plimsolls, and running the half a mile up the lane to check on the tree house we had made the day before in a great beech set in a woodland glade. I would have been no more than seven years old.

Every expedition was accompanied by dogs, and 'taking the dogs for a walk' was also a specific job doled out by my mother as one of a check-list of chores that had to be done. Chop wood, fill the coal scuttles, feed the chickens, wash up, lay the next meal, tidy your room, gather vegetables for lunch, mow the lawn, weed the strawberries, turn the compost – the list always lengthened when the garden became involved. So walking the dogs, which I loved, became the soft option. I learned to complain a little so as not to give away the fact I actively wanted to do it, but in fact my mother did not care. She just wanted the jobs done and exercising the dogs was, to her, just another rather lengthy, time-consuming chore among a day made up of little other than obligations stacked one on the other.

So I would walk for hours, sometimes alone but more often than not with one of my brothers or sisters, cousins – I was related to half the village – or a friend with at least two dogs roaming unchecked.

The dogs of my childhood overlapped and merge in memory, yet each was an integral member of the family. There was Meg, my grandmother's corgi, who waddled round the garden and never came for a walk. She would yap until Granny would shout 'Where's the whip?!' and Meg would sullenly beat a rotund retreat.

Maada was a yellow Labrador that arrived in the spring of 1960, named after the initials of us five children in ascending age (Montagu, Alison, Andrew, David and Anthea). I was four, nearly five. She arrived sitting in a cardboard Bird's Custard box and slept in a bed under the kitchen dresser. My mother said, 'Be careful, she has teeth like needles' and I wondered whether a mouth full of needles hurt her. I would often crawl under the dresser and curl up in her bed with her.

When Maada was just ten months old she had a litter of pups sired by the Dalmatian across the road. The result was twelve black puppies with white blazes and stars. My father drowned four of them in a bucket. He said that Maada could not cope with them all. She was too young. I seem to remember that this was an accepted practice and considered good husbandry. The fact that they were mongrels and effectively worthless might also have had something to do with it. For a long time I would look at the three buckets in the pantry and wonder which one he had used.

Maada and the pups were ensconced in the playhouse that my father had built for my twin sister and me. It remained a kennel-cum-store-shed but it seemed a fair swap. A shed full of pups with their fat tummies and warm biscuity smell was better than any token Wendy house.

A week after the pups were born there was a storm. Maada, scarcely more than a pup herself, took each of her babies by the loose scruff of the neck, and carried them one by one up through the garden in the lightning and torrential rain to the back door. When about four were there, she barked and barked until let in and the puppies dried and rescued. We put them all under the dresser, wrapped in blankets.

A few years later Maada had another litter with a pedigree Labrador. This time all were allowed to live and all were sold for what was then a good price – about twenty pounds. The last two to go were sisters, Vicky and Vanny. Lie on your back and they would crawl over you, nibbling your nose and pulling your socks. My twin sister and I wept when they left, feeling something was lost. But these pups were never ours. We borrowed them for eight to ten weeks. But when you are an eight year old, eight weeks is as much a span of life as you can hold at any time.

Bengy the beagle was my mother's dog. She still delegated taking him for a walk. However, it was one thing to take him off for a walk, but quite another to bring him back. He would disappear hunting for hours – sometimes days – and then return with muddy feet, bounding up the stairs and on to the bed. Indoors he was as sweet a dog as any I have known, charming, fun and gentle. But once outside, every fibre of his being wanted to be away and follow the scent wherever and however long it took him.

Then a black Labrador called Sam appeared. He overlapped Maada and Maada overlapped Bengy and I spent half my waking hours walking or playing with them. I never tired of the immediate and particular countryside around the village, never lost wonder at the way that it changed through the seasons. The farm that made up most of the land was mixed, with small tractors pulling the plough for months at a time, and frisky bullocks charging after the dogs as we raced to the safety of the gate, snatching the dogs with us.

Great flocks of partridges scurried low over the stubble fields and we would find their nests in spring in a scrape among the emerging green wheat across which hares zigzagged. Pheasants cackled and exploded out of the hedges everywhere. Occasionally one of our dogs would emerge with one in its mouth. Although we knew that this was technically poaching, it seemed fair game and it would be taken home, plucked and eaten. We mushroomed in early autumn and tobogganed in January, waded waist high through the hay in June and prickled our bare shins on the stubble in August.

We roamed untrammelled, children and dogs, taking each other for walks. There were barn owls in the ruined farm at the far end of the lane, which slid soundlessly from the upstairs bedroom through the broken window and out to where the old man's beard smothered the trees at the woodland edge. The chalk pit had badgers we never saw and there were rats in the rick where the lane forked. And sometimes there were Red Indians galloping over the horizon and goblins hiding in the elms.

When I was seven I was sent away to boarding school. Life changed. Home became the place I went for my holidays. It was an absence, a heartache, where all the things I loved lived.

About five days before the end of each school holiday, completely ruining the last week, my mother would get out my trunk and start to fill it, slowly mending, adding name tapes, and occasionally taking me on shopping trips to replace parts of the uniform. This would send the dogs into gloom and they would often get into the trunk, lying on the rolled socks (knee-length, grey), ironed shirts (flannel, grey) or vests (winter). When it was actually time to go and I appeared in my itchy flannel suit with short trousers and cap and the car was packed with trunk and wooden tuck box, the dogs would not leave their bed or raise their heads, knowing that whatever jaunt I was going on excluded them. And for me the pang of not seeing them for twelve weeks grieved me every bit as much as not seeing my parents.

7. The Keepers

Walking the dogs in my childhood was a pleasure that was always qualified by the Keepers.

The Keepers, as we always knew them, were Mr Brown and Mr Brown, father and son, who were gamekeepers for the estate that owned the farm and woods. They policed them officiously, patrolling in a Land Rover that was the only vehicle that ever used these lanes. We would see it parked in a ride, or emerging at the crest of a slope, and duck the other side of a hedge while it went past. Occasionally they would find us and we had to brazen it out, pretending that the dogs were always under control.

In spring the pheasant eggs were hatched and by early summer there were thousands of chicks in loose pens in the woods. The Mr Browns would come and feed them daily and shoot anything that might eat them. We found gibbets of stoats, weasels, crows, magpies, jays, sparrowhawks, kestrels, all hung on the spikes of a barbed wire fence in long grisly rows, along with scores of moles – not that moles could have posed much threat to the baby pheasants.

By late summer these hand-reared birds were released into the landscape, where they pottered around rather dozily until the shooting season started at the beginning of October. The partridge season began a month earlier, and lasted only as long as there was stubble on the ground.

Most Saturdays throughout winter the gunfire would begin around nine o'clock, break for lunch and then continue until dusk. Walking the dogs on these days was out of the question. Then, on the first of February, the season was over and we emerged from the trenches, knowing that there was a brief period before the pheasants started breeding and the temporary pens in the woods would start to fill up with pheasant chicks and become a kind of minefield for us and our dogs.

But there was one beneficial side effect to this obsession with game shooting. It had preserved the landscape. After the Second World War British agriculture became dramatically more industrialised, and bigger and bigger tractors replaced the previous teams of horses that had plodded up and down these fields. In the 1960s and '70s thousands of miles of hedgerows were ripped out to form vast fields that suited the new intensive grain production. In many parts of Hampshire the landscape, including an area just a few miles from our village, was reduced to an undulating prairie devoid of a hedge or single tree and, as herbicides became more prevalent, devoid of any plant at all other than the sown crop. They quickly came to house the ecosystem of a concrete yard. I have been to the Midwest prairies of Kansas and they can be magnificently beautiful, but these ripped-apart farms had none of their grandeur or scale.

So the shape and body of the countryside that I grew up with and learned to love was grace and favour of the guns that paid highly to slaughter the carefully reared birds. There was more than a moral sting in the tail. Those guns paid highly for their shooting rights and in return expected birds – lots and lots of birds – to go up after each drive. In short, the Keepers' jobs depended entirely upon that supply being abundant between 1 October and 1 February. Anything that diminished that supply, including the Dons' uncontrolled dogs, was a threat to their livelihood and the roof over their heads. These were the days when all estate workers lived in tied cottages. Lose your job for whatever reason and you also lost your home. I considered none of this at the time and saw them only as the enemy – but hindsight looks back with a less polarised eye.

One night the phone in the hall rang at ten. The phone never rang after nine p.m. except in emergencies. In fact, until then this was only an unspoken principle. In my short life there had never been a late-night emergency. But that day Bengy had gone hunting and taken Maada with him, and although we had all walked every lane calling and whistling and rattling leads, night fell and there were no dogs. In itself, that was a kind of emergency.

The voice on the phone belonged to the elder Mr Brown. 'We've got your dogs. Collect them now or I will shoot them.'

My father put on his overcoat with his cheque book in one pocket and two leads in the other and drove off to the pair of Keepers' cottages at the edge of the woods. It appeared that the two dogs had got into a breeding pen and created havoc, causing the death of scores of birds. When a cheque to cover the loss of profit from the guns was handed over, the dogs were exchanged. Mr Brown made it clear that the next phone call would be for us to collect their bodies.

For a few weeks after that all walks were conducted with the dogs permanently on a lead. But then this regime was softened so they would be allowed to run in a safe field, and later in the lanes, and before long the leads would only be put on when we saw the Land Rover in the distance.

Inevitably it happened again. The dogs went off and night came. We did not wait for the call but rang the Keepers. They had both dogs, caught before they could do any damage but effectively trespassing. They had not shot them – yet. But this time the younger Mr Brown said that he would shoot them if he even saw them off a lead. He meant it.

My father said that the old man was just doing his job. But the son was a B. I was not sure what a B was, but guessed it was Bad.

So the Keepers became ogres in this lovely countryside, and every horizon, every gap between the trees was scoured for signs of the green Land Rover with the ubiquitous shotgun leaning back between the two front seats.

Now the leads were used in earnest and Bengy, the lovely beagle with insatiable wanderlust, was kept indoors or, increasingly, chained up to a tree for most of the day. A few times he escaped, to be retrieved from another part of the county after desperately anxious nights. Then, after one particularly long escape – I seem to remember it was two whole days – my parents had him put down rather than either keeping him chained up or having him shot in the night.

It was the only time I ever saw my mother cry.

At the time it seemed one of those inexplicably cruel adult decisions. But there was a logic to it. Better to take a loved animal to the vet, to hold him or her in your arms as they are painlessly put to sleep and to bury them in the garden than have them shot in the dark like vermin.

In the dormitory at school I used to dream that I was wandering the lanes, calling his name hopelessly, and then finding Bengy's body hung on the barbed wire along with the stoats and crows.

8. The Back Yard
and The Spring Garden

When we arrived at Longmeadow in the autumn of 1991, the back yard was the only part that was not either abandoned, overgrown field or piled with building rubble. This was the garden.

It is not big – some thirty feet wide and fifteen feet deep – with a brick floor. Not that we knew this when we came because the bricks were under an inch or two of soil and matted grass.

Originally the wall, which we raised a little, would have existed to keep animals out yet be visible. It now serves to keep dogs contained but in fresh air if need be, and as a kind of horticultural boot room, with a stone sink for washing vegetables and a stone table that was once a slab for salting bacon. The washing line is strung across it with a bean stick cut from the coppice propping it up. There is a well in the corner, still with water in it, going down to a water table that even in the driest months is still quite high.

There are a couple of figs trained against the wall, one of which bears delicious fruit and the other a little less giving but handsome enough; mint growing in the corner trapped by brickwork, and lots of pots of Mediterranean herbs that can have the sharp drainage they crave and be within easy reach of the kitchen. In summer there are lots of pelargoniums too. In winter the stone table serves as a bird table, and the gold-finches and long-tailed tits come in flocks and bustle between the blackbirds; occasionally a sparrowhawk will turn at right angles round the building, swoop in and lift one from the table before perching on the wall with its prize, panting with triumph.

As well as being a suntrap, it is also always dry underfoot, even in the middle of a wet winter in this fundamentally wet place.

But only just. We have had the floods licking at the bricks of the yard, to the extent that we have put sandbags under the back door because if the water gets in the yard then it is only an inch from getting into the house.

But to Nigel it is the portal to the garden and walks, and even just stepping into it promises fun. And it is his dining room. Come rain, wind or snow, Nigel is always fed outside in the back yard. Which means that in his eyes this, with the central stone path that has continued from the cars down between the yews in the front, through the front door, down the hall, through the back kitchen and on out to here, this is the culmination of the stone path and his dining room and, for Nigel, the loveliest part of the entire garden.

The yard outside the back door is enclosed by a brick wall with two wooden doors. One leads to the Spring Garden; if Nigel is in a meditative mood he gently meanders down the curving path made from quarry tiles, half-bricks, roofing tiles, concrete blocks and cobbles – all the bits and pieces of building waste left over from the repair of the house and that we did not have the heart to smash up and make into hardcore over twenty-five years ago – sniffing snowdrops and hellebores in February and March, pulmonarias, tellima, tiarella, fritillaries and daffodils around Easter, 'Spring Green' and 'West Point' tulips at the end of April and into May, with the foxy rankness of the imperial fritillaries, growing like demented pineapples, muscling other scents aside, and the electric green of euphorbia and the emerging foliage setting the senses tingling.

By the end of May it is a green and shady place and Nigel has to shoulder his way through the cow parsley that rises like surf above all else. When this dies down and the canopy of the trees is closed above, the Spring Garden goes dormant and becomes very dry, almost unrecognisable from the flooded, fecund slice of ground that holds all the first flowers at the beginning of the year.

9. Breakfast

Nigel watches me eat my breakfast with mounting interest. I like a leisurely breakfast with three distinct courses (yoghurt and stewed fruit, eggs of some kind, toast and marmalade, and a large pot of tea since you ask), and like to read at least one newspaper as I eat. All this takes fully half an hour and Nigel has learned to pace himself. In the very early days, when he was a small puppy, there was the outrage that I was clearly eating something delicious and not sharing it with him. But he quickly learned that he was not welcome at the table and that sitting by my chair with strings of drool hanging from his mouth was not going to endear himself to me or anyone else. So he lies in his too-small bed and watches from under the lid of one eye.

Nigel watches me eat like someone viewing a (rather dull and slightly messy) food programme that he has seen a hundred times before but finds comforting. He knows the script by heart. Yoghurt down, bowl put on the side. Noted. Eggs to be cooked. Play it cool. Stretch, exhale deeply, show no interest what, so, ever. Eggs eaten, very good. Moving nicely forward. A second cup of tea is a blow, slowing down everything. Toast, get the butter; out of marmalade so a trip to the larder for apricot jam. Into the last lap now.

He watches me meaningfully, catching my eye, and risks a wag of his tail thumping against the wooden sides of his bed. All done? Ready to feed the troops now? No hurry, of course. In your own time. It's just that I do feel a trifle peckish . . .

What! A *third* cup of tea?! Oh come on!

At this point he gets up, nudges my elbow, makes an unmanly high-pitched bleat that drops into a growl, stretches, looks meaningfully at the door to the back kitchen where his food is kept, and will grasp my tea-drinking hand as if to lug me forcibly away from my own, overplayed breakfast towards his own.

Nigel only gets fed one meal a day, first thing in the morning. Before he goes to bed at night there are biscuits, quite a lot of biscuits, every scrap eaten with intense delight, but that counts as a snack rather than a meal. Breakfast is the real thing. Serious stuff. He is not a greedy dog, just hungry. I had a Labrador for ten years that was a paragon of all virtue save for an overriding, cunning, insatiable greed. Nigel knows restraint and has, to my knowledge, never stolen any food in his life, but by breakfast time he has a fierce appetite.

The rituals are well established. His food is kept in a metal dustbin which in itself is an object of veneration and fear. Breakfast lives in it, which makes it a very good thing indeed, but it makes an alarming noise when moved and, much worse, has a lid and Nigel doesn't like lids. Or the colour orange. Or hats. Or any stick held above waist level that could turn into a gun which could make a truly terrifying noise. So lifting the lid is a scary delight.

Nigel eats special food for sensitive skin. Like many golden retrievers, Nigel has all kinds of problems with his skin, which is sensitive and often very itchy. Long grass can irritate it, although we are surrounded by long grass. Getting wet is also unhelpful, but it rains most of the time and Nigel lives to swim or immerse himself in a puddle. Warm, damp weather makes it worse – but the general trend is for the weather to become warmer and damper all year round. We have tried every permutation of diet, steroids and homeopathic treatment, but it is a problem that never quite goes away and occasionally flares up into something quite serious.

It usually begins with a cut or abrasion, which becomes a 'hot spot' and very quickly develops into an open sore. Nigel will scratch and rub at this, making it much worse, and often the first sign that he has real skin problems is the sight of him rubbing his face on the ground while making loud grunting and groaning noises. He loves frosty ground the most for this, which can be really abrasive and cause nasty skin burns – so that sound is now always a signal to find him and stop the scratching by distracting him with a ball. We have learned to check him regularly and treat any tiny skin wound immediately with cortisone cream to stop it developing. However, on one memorably tragic occasion it got so bad that Nigel had to have his head shaved and wear a protective veterinary collar to stop him scratching. It was very sad and quite funny to everyone except poor Nigel, who looked bizarre and more akin to an unfledged bird than a proud canine warrior with flowing golden locks. But it all grew back and has never had to be repeated.

Nigel sits talking to me as I prepare his breakfast. There is a waiting-for-food range of noises that rise from a hurry-up growl to a high-pitched plea. If he thinks I am being unreasonably slow, an irritated bark will be thrown in, followed by an apologetic shuffle of his backside. He is fundamentally a polite dog – albeit one getting hungrier by the second. Finally meat is added and mixed and I lift his metal bowl off the counter and, unlike all the other dogs I have fed, he ignores me and the food and prances – no, *dances* – to the door to the yard without a backward glance. He knows the form. He has learned the ropes and is one step ahead. The bowl is put in front of him whereupon he sits and looks with quiet desperation at me while a bubble of saliva gently balloons from the corner of his mouth, and on the command he tucks in. I know when he has finished by the sound of the empty metal bowl scraping over the uneven bricks as he licks the last traces from it.

And so it happens every day, exactly the same every time. But every time is the best time.

10. The Lime Walk

Although the back yard has been there for centuries and connects the back kitchen to the house in a practical and useful way, the Lime Walk is our main route out into the garden. Neither the door to it nor the path itself existed before we came. In fact, had a door been there, it would have opened on to an area where pigs were kept, with a wall, beyond which was a rough field.

The house is in one corner of the rectangular plot at Longmeadow. The Spring Garden, Lime Walk and Long Walk run across the site, but everything else is based along the length of the garden, away and at right angles to the house.

The Lime Walk was the first of these cross paths to be made. I had bid on job lots of *Tilia platyphyllos* and *T. cordata*, among other things, in a tree sale back in April 1993, without really keeping a reckoning on what I was buying or thinking where or how I was going to plant them. However, they were going at ridiculously cheap prices – fifty pence for a ten-foot lime – and it struck me as an opportunity not to be missed. The fact that I neither had the money in my account to pay for them nor any means of getting more money from any source was a slight problem, but it was a Saturday, I reckoned the cheque would not be presented till Tuesday at the earliest, so I had forty-eight hours to borrow the money. Which I did.

Limes pleach very well and, given that I had over a hundred of them, I needed to plant them as close together as possible, so originally the Spring, Cottage and Jewel gardens each had a surround of pleached limes which created pleached avenues between them. Hence the Lime Walk.

Sarah gave me forty yards' worth of old bricks for my fortieth birthday and these became the path. I planted 'White Triumphator' tulips down both sides as well as *Alchemilla mollis* and, at various times over the years, white foxgloves and *Nicotiana sylvestris*. We have recently planted *Dryopteris filix-mas* ferns under the limes and they love the cool shade and look tremendous, especially in winter. The limes that were more slender than the stakes that supported them have become thick-trunked trees and the path has dipped and buckled over the years. I like that.

I like the walk and its view a lot. I like it when the bottom half is flooded, which happens a few times every year, and I like the cool shade the limes create in high summer. But most of all I like the way that it invites me on and out into the garden, with the promise of so much more when, halfway along its length, you look left and the central path runs unexpectedly far from you.

Nigel likes it as a doggy bowling alley. You have to stand at the door and roll the ball underarm as straight as possible so that it does not bounce into the borders. Not that the tennis ball does any harm, but the charging retriever crashes through the plants destroying a swathe of gardening in his wake, before wheeling back triumphantly for it all to happen again.

11. Gretel

The first dog that was truly my own was a Labrador called Gretel.

A week before my twenty-first birthday I carried her home across the fields. She could fit in one of my hands. I chose her from a litter of ten pups because she seemed the most vivacious. 'A little monster,' the owner had said. For some reason I thought of Grendel, the monster from *Beowulf*. But Grendel seemed an unfortunate name for this beautiful little pup so it was softened to Gretel. The name stuck.

Gretel was very responsive and quickly bonded closely with me. By the time she was about six months old I wanted to train her so she would retrieve properly. Looking back it was odd that I should choose a dog bred primarily for retrieving dead birds, when the whole regime of shooting had caused such problems with our other dogs.

That Christmas I was drinking in the local pub with Gretel sitting at my feet. She grew to love pubs and would quickly learn a routine that involved finding someone eating crisps and sitting staring at them with an orphaned, longing gaze. There were no such thing as gastropubs in those days, and public bars were smoke-fugged and mostly occupied by men drinking pints of bitter, but wives and girlfriends would be seated and treated to the luxury of a packet of crisps or nuts or, maybe, if things were really wild, a pickled egg from the big jar on the bar. Gretel, who like all Labradors liked her food, would work her way round the pub following the crackle of crisp packets.

A thickset man was leaning against the bar with his back to me. When he turned I saw it was the younger Mr Brown.

'New dog I see.'

I bristled. I was a grown-up, after a fashion, played rugby, worked on a building site, could handle myself. But he still had all the authority. He looked me up and down and then at Gretel, lying quietly at my feet.

'Dog or bitch?'

'Bitch.'

'Nice-looking dog.' I realised that he was not eyeing up her potential as a pheasant killer but as a working animal, just as a shepherd might assess a young collie. 'Going to work her?' he said.

Although I had not given it a moment's thought, I heard myself say that I was and that I intended to shoot with her.

Then Mr Brown, the terror on the horizon and spoiler of walks, looked me in the eye, seemed to make a decision, and for the next ten minutes spoke wisely and kindly on how best to train a young dog to retrieve. I was to apply all the same lessons when training Nigel – but that was over a quarter of century later.

I loved the process of training Gretel. It was the first time I had ever worked with an animal. The 'with' was the key. She wanted to retrieve and wanted to please. She was astonishingly good at it. All I had to do was channel that enthusiasm to where I wanted it to be at any particular time. The magic words were 'Go on'. They were the trigger that released her to do what she wanted more than anything else.

Despite my claim to Mr Brown – said, I suspect, to ingratiate myself with him – I never did go shooting with Gretel, so she was not a proper working dog. But we developed an almost telepathic relationship and I rarely had to say anything. A look or a nod would be enough. Her obedience was expressed more in pubs and streets – knowing she would not stray or be distracted – but we had party tricks based on those early training days. If we were walking along the lanes I would drop my handkerchief without showing her and walk another ten minutes. Then all I had to do was murmur 'Go on' and she would shoot straight back the way we came and reappear – always – with the hanky in her mouth.

Although I suspect there was a rule somewhere forbidding it, I had Gretel with me all the time I was at university, and no one seemed to mind unduly. I would take her for a walk at dawn going along the river east one day to Fen Ditton and west to Grantchester meadows the next. The latter meant walking through the empty streets of Cambridge at five in the morning, and it never looked or seemed more entrancing or more of a privilege to be there.

I would never leave her for more than a couple of hours and she went wherever I went; if she was unwelcome, I would absent myself. As it turned out I only went to about half a dozen lectures in three years, preferring to take books from the library and read in my rooms with Gretel curled up at my feet.

She came to parties, working the room just as she would a pub, but always materialising when it was time to go home – and more often than not she would lead a tipsy me back home. I also had a cockerel for a while, which used to come along too. I remember leaning over Magdalene Bridge in the middle of the night, Gretel sitting patiently and the cockerel perched on the parapet, nodding with sleep. Suddenly he lifted his head and crowed with full voice, filling the empty streets with a sound that cannot have been heard there for a long, long time.

When I walked around Cambridge Gretel would wander with me, never on a lead but easily keeping pace without ever having to be told to heel or stay with me. If I went into a shop I would leave her sitting outside and she was always still there when I came out again – sometimes, if browsing books, over half an hour later. This is unthinkable now, but forty years ago it was perfectly possible if, even back then, considered a little unusual.

The only thing Gretel could not resist was a butcher's. If we passed one she would clock it with a single turn of her head and a sudden flash of longing in her eyes but keep walking, assuming that I had not noticed. But if I stopped to chat or look in a window she would shoot back and I would find her standing outside longingly, drooling and looking in at the sawdust-floored shop – back then all butchers scattered fresh sawdust every day on the shop floor to soak up any blood – where large men with unnaturally ruddy faces cut and carved joints of meat on great chopping blocks scalloped with use. I would buy a marrowbone for ten pence, which she would carry back and busy herself with for days.

I shared a house with a veterinary student who had obtained the carcass of a fallow deer and painstakingly skinned and dismembered it in our tiny kitchen, boiled it limb by limb, head and all, and removed all the soft tissue to end up with a bag of bones which he then painstakingly assembled as part of his anatomy studies. He was unsurprisingly extremely proud of the resulting skeleton, linked by wires, which hung like a puppet in his room. Gretel had clearly bathed in the delicious smells that accompanied all the various stages of dismemberment and cooking and bided her time. One day Alastair must have left his door open because Gretel was found surrounded by half-eaten bones and the wreckage of a deer skeleton. He never forgave her or, I think, me.

Sarah and I eloped to the North York Moors in the autumn of 1979. I was a recently graduated student and Sarah was married to someone else. We set off in Sarah's 2CV with a few bits of furniture, lots of books and Gretel. Sarah says that she knew I really loved her the first time I called her Gretel by mistake. We were house-sitting for a distant cousin, the rent being to paint the windows and ride his horse every day to keep it fit for hunting. I had painted lots of windows in my time, which was just as well as the house had lots of windows to be painted, but had never sat on a horse before. This one, Countess, was a seventeen-hands, bad-tempered Cleveland Bay. I would saddle her up, clamber on and set off across the astonishingly beautiful North York Moors above the little village of Lealholm. It was a good way to learn how to ride. We were as stubborn as each other and most rides were a process of seeing whose will would break first. But occasionally we both surrendered to the wills and whims of the other and I had some sublime moments when horse and rider became one exhilarated gallop across the heather with Gretel running alongside. When we broke from a canter to a gallop, Gretel would always react as though a trigger had been pressed, and change with us from a lope to a tongue-lolling, ears-back gallop herself, straining everything to keep up, but part of that exhilaration too.

The moors were a new and strange landscape for me who had been brought up in the rolling, soft countryside of Hampshire. But I liked their silence and stillness and scale, with the eye drawn to the far, unbroken horizon and the houses hunkered down in the dales with which they were corrugated.

September and October were the height of the grouse-shooting season; the moors that began a quarter of a mile behind our house and ran all the way to Whitby and Robin Hood's Bay to the east and to Kirkbymoorside and Pickering in the south were maintained for – and as a result of – the business of running the grouse shoots.

There is much to be said against grouse shooting, not least

in the destruction of rare and beautiful raptors like the hen harrier, merlin and short-eared owl who share the moorland habitat and are seen as enemies of grouse chicks. One might also object to the morality of driving reared birds to be systematically slaughtered for fun. But where grouse shooting has not been maintained, neither have the moors, with their complex and subtle ecosystem based upon specific heights and stages of growth of heather, and it does provide important employment locally as well as providing perfectly legal sport for the shooters.

So at the beginning of October, Sarah and I joined the dozen or so 'bud drivers' in the back of an old van to be driven to the first drive, where we fanned out in a long line and walked noisily through the heather towards the butts on the horizon, rousing the grouse before us.

The pay for the day was £6.50 and a bottle of beer. We bought our sandwiches for lunch. Our other bud drivers were local farmers happy to have a day out in the autumnal sun. They chattered away to each other as we lurched down the moorland tracks across Danby High Moor. They might as well have been talking Romanian for all that Sarah and I understood. The combination of the broad North Yorkshire accent and the local Cleveland dialect was another language entirely. Robert, our neighbouring farmer, who took us under his wise and wily wing, explained. 'When we tak to yow, we spake pink. So you understand like. But when us spake to yin another we tak the way we allus do like.'

Gretel came with us to help drive the grouse, which would whirr up from the heather like missiles, sometimes waiting until you were almost treading on them with their distinctive 'Goback goback goback' cry of alarm. The guns, almost all Dutch or German, with their handmade tweed suits, thick brogues and very thick dogs, missed nearly all of them. The ones that they did hit fell hundreds of yards from them, instantly lost in the heather. The dogs would then be sent out to pick them up. Very soon I saw that of the half-dozen dogs that had been brought along, only a couple were any use at all and the rest almost uncontrollable. Gretel sat by my side watching with a mixture of curiosity and contempt. At lunch I suggested that she might be able to help. So, at the next drive, after waiting for the other dogs to fail again, I sent her off. She immediately found one bird, brought it back and then went off again and picked up another. There was not much thanks for this, given that all it did was show up the lack of expertise of the very expensively trained dogs the guests had brought along. But for the rest of the week Gretel cleared up behind them.

While she was a paragon of obedience, responsiveness and the best possible companion, Gretel was incorrigibly greedy and a thief to boot.

One Christmas, when we were staying with my parents, we went out visiting and left the dogs at home. When we came back it was tea-time and we looked everywhere for the Christmas cake. This was a large, fully iced affair that my mother made each year as an annual performance and was always decorated with the same mixture of Father Christmas, a snowman, a robin on a spring and an angel. A glittery, holly-printed cake band wrapped around it to add the final tasteful touch. But it was nowhere to be found. The plate that it was on was there, spotlessly clean. We looked at the dogs. My father's terrier growled resentfully. Gretel beamed and wagged her tale gently, clearly free from the tiniest stain of guilt. There were no crumbs, no torn bits of cake band, no sign of cake-larceny whatsoever. It was a complete mystery.

A week later, when Sarah and I had returned back to London, Gretel was looking uncomfortable and wanted to be let out into the garden. A few minutes later there was the customary polite bark at the door as she asked to be let back in, clearly easier in stride. And in the middle of the lawn there was an extra-large pile of dog poo with a robin on a spring balanced on its top.

For ten years Gretel was my constant companion. Sarah, who was not in the least fond of dogs when I met her, but who realised very soon that if she were to love me then she had to love my dogs too, grew to adore her as well. We were a household.

The house we lived in was the end of terrace in Ufton Road, in what was then a rundown area called De Beauvoir, caught in the no man's land between Islington and Hackney. We were able to buy it because of the insalubrious area, lack of public transport and inconvenience for everywhere except the City and Islington. We did not realise how lucky we were back then, buying a three-storey town house within walking distance of both the Angel and Old Street roundabout, in our mid-twenties. It is unthinkable now, and was only possible for us back then because my grandfather died and left me some stocks and shares. When I sold them – within an hour of receiving the certificates – I had seven thousand pounds to put down as a deposit. Nowadays that would hardly pay the estate agent's fee.

The house was divided erratically into two flats, one made up of absurdly small rooms, the other encrusted with 1960s DIY. It had what the agents crushingly called 'potential'. But the garden was extra-large, with an L-shaped section at the end that had once belonged to the adjoining house. This – and the rest of the terrace – had been flattened by bombs in the war and the two gardens had been combined.

The size emphasised how little there was in it other than some scanty grass and a few apologetic shrubs planted much too close to the edge. But it made a perfect football pitch for Gretel, and in the first winter I spent hours kicking a ball past her so she could run down to the end of the garden, retrieve it and plonk it back at my feet for another go.

As the weather warmed in the spring of 1982, I began digging to make borders. In fact it took nearly six months and two full skips to clear the ground. I learned later that the previous owner had repaired and sold old cars and it seemed that he got rid of all the redundant parts by burying them in his back garden. So, intending to till the soil, I ended up excavating piston heads, door panels, wing mirrors, roof racks, camshafts and carburettors, as well as a building site's worth of bricks and hardcore. Gretel's football pitch became earthworks.

But eventually the garden could come into being. Over the next few years Gretel's playground was transformed into four separate areas.

Immediately outside the back door we had a paved yard with raised beds bounded by low brick walls just the right height for sitting on. In summer we had a table in this yard that served both as a potting bench and dining table. An eight-foot brick wall made this area a square, and we had a specially made oak lattice door, through which you passed into an area of two wide borders with a flagged path down the centre.

The west-facing boundary was made up of a thirty-foot-high blank brick wall that was the rear of a factory making sheet metal; this created a superb backdrop for climbing roses, clematis, wisteria and honeysuckle. On the other, shadier side there was a nature reserve filled with tall trees behind our fencing. It was screened, private and sheltered. The path led to a small flagged square where we had another table that was bathed in evening light, where we often ate our supper, carrying trays of food down the garden path, with Gretel eagerly following, ready to help out if we felt that there was too much on our plates . . . Then off at right angles was another area that you could not see until you reached the seating area at the end that was the size of many a back garden, which we grassed and planted with flanking fruit trees under-planted with bulbs. It was bounded by another workshop with high brick walls. We thought it was heaven.

Every weekend and summer evening, Sarah and I would spend most of our time out there, dirty, messy, happy and accompanied always by Gretel and then, when he came along, Eric the terrier – usually clutching half a brick.

Gretel was ten when she got cancer. She had slowed down a little and had a cough. I took her to the vet who looked a little concerned – probably nothing, but best to check – and said he would like to do an X-ray. When I went back to collect her he looked me in the eye and said, 'I'm very sorry . . .'

I drove to the vet with Gretel sitting in the passenger seat next to me. She sat up and looked around and then lay with her head on my lap. I held her in my arms as the vet gave her the injection. She gave a little huff and stopped breathing. I had put her bed and a shovel in the back of the car and carried her out and curled her up in her bed. I then drove the fifty miles to a field I'd once owned in Hampshire.

I had turned twenty-one during the blazing summer of 1976. I was working on a building site and we started at 6.30 a.m. to try and get as much done before it got too hot. At 5.30 both my parents came into my bedroom and my father threw an envelope on the bed. In it were the deeds for a two-acre field called Charles' Acre. Through a convoluted chain of events my father had acquired it in the 1950s from a cousin of my mother's in an attempt to have a stake in what was almost completely my mother's territory. It never worked and he always felt an outsider, never taking any interest in the field. But I loved it, and the reality of owning a piece of land in the landscape I loved was overwhelming.

Seven years later I gave it back to him. I had got behind on repayments for money I owed him for a car I'd bought off him. I knew he was near death, so when he wrote the repayments off – it was a few hundred – I returned the deeds of the field and said he should leave it to my brother in his will. I don't know why I did that because I loved it, other than cutting free. Letting go.

When Gretel died I asked my brother if I could bury her in the field, so I drove straight to it, left her in the car and walked to the top of the hill with my shovel and dug a grave with a view out over the Hampshire countryside we had both loved. It was the last week of November, the countryside stripped bare. A weak sun paling the barley stubble.

Once through the first foot of topsoil, it was almost pure chalk and hard digging. I remember the chalk streaked pink from the blood on my hands as blisters became raw, bleeding sores. I felt nothing.

I carried her up the hill – learning for the first time the meaning of a dead weight. Already, after just a few hours, she had the slight whiff of death. I went back down and brought up the bed, her food dish, a bag of food and a favourite ball. She lay curled up in her wicker bed at the bottom of the five-foot shaft of chalk, a bowl of food prepared just as she liked it and a ball. When she woke, I thought, she will be hungry. The ball will comfort her. When she woke she would not be confused but know where she was and be free to run in familiar fields.

Then I threw the spoil back over her, worked fast, refilling the hole, piling the excess in a chalky mound and topping it with lumps of glassy black flint.

When it was all done, hands bloodied and raw to the meat, I sat down and wept for my dog, my father and my field. And myself. When I finally walked down in the dark I knew that everything that connected me to this place was now over.

I had buried my past.

12. A Brief History of the Golden Retriever

Until the nineteenth century, dogs were defined not so much by breed but by what they did. So guard dogs were categorised into those that barked and those that bit and, refined even further, those that bit before they barked or those that barked first and bit later. Hounds, the most prized of all dogs, were divided into ones that chased and those that used their noses to flush the prey out. Spaniels retrieved, pointers pointed and setters set, but it was the skills of the dog that grouped it into a type rather than the details of its appearance. This meant that they made, by modern standards, a fairly motley crew, and although some breeds, like foxhounds, whippets or toy spaniels, are recognisably similar, others barely fit our concept of what certain breeds ought to look like at all.

It was nineteenth- and twentieth-century urban life and the general sophistication of modern society that categorised dogs into standardised breeds. The first dog show was held in Newcastle in 1859 and the Kennel Club was founded in 1873 and, in 1891, an employee of the famous Spratt's dog biscuits, Charles Cruft, began what was to become the most celebrated dog show in the world.

The irony of this is that the less dogs were actually used, the more strictly the definitions of their uses became policed. If we were to parachute back two or three hundred years, most dogs would be more or less mongrels, although those belonging to the gentry or farmers would have had dominant characteristics that were carefully encouraged through selective breeding with bloodlines highly valued. But they would be thought of as coming from a certain place or person rather than being an independent breed that – heaven forbid – the common classes could appreciate or employ.

Golden retrievers evolved as a distinctive breed as a direct result of the late nineteenth-century obsession with game shooting and, slightly more circuitously, with the development of the breech-loading shotgun.

The transition from muzzle loaders to breech loaders

gradually took place throughout the nineteenth century. However, they did not become commonplace among sportsmen until breech loaders became as light and accurate as the muzzle loaders that had been in use since the late seventeenth century. Refinements to the technology involving cartridges, hammer and cartridge ejection over the following decades meant that by the late 1880s the modern side-by-side shotgun was universal among sportsmen.

One of the results of this was that game shooting changed from an activity done by individuals or shared by a small group to the huge, highly organised shoots of the late Victorian period, where thousands of birds could be shot in a single short winter's day slaughter.

The sport became hugely significant as a measure of social class. One of the ways that new money, usually made as a result of the despised trade or industry, could become socially acceptable was to spend it on a country estate, where the new rich could set themselves and their children up as landed gentry (which coincidentally meant laying out parks and gardens as another indicator of new-found rank). Having got their estate by the middle of the nineteenth century, it was essential to have a well-run shoot, employing gamekeepers to rear the pheasants, partridges and, on the moors of northern England and Scotland, grouse. 'Rearing' involved as much policing of every and any creature that might harm the precious sporting harvest, so anything that might prey on them from egg to mature bird was ruthlessly eliminated.

'The shoot' became a parade of subtle social niceties, including wearing the right clothes, using the right weapon, showing the right shooting prowess and exhibiting the right social behaviour as a guest at the house parties that invariably accompanied the shoots. And, significantly, being accompanied by the right kind of dog trained in the right way.

One of the upshots of these changes was that more and more birds were falling, dead or mortally wounded, in awkward and inaccessible places, including water. Better and more specifically equipped gundogs that had the retrieving instinct yet were bigger and stronger – and in particular good strong swimmers – than the ubiquitous spaniel were needed to retrieve them.

The origin of golden retrievers is subject to some debate, but most agree that the modern dog begins when Sir Dudley Coutts Marjoribanks, Lord Tweedmouth, crossed a male yellow wavy-coated retriever called Nous in 1868 with a Tweed water spaniel bitch called Belle, resulting in three puppies called – and the names are a clue to the colours – Primrose, Crocus and Cowslip.

What is subject to much debate in certain quarters is what exactly the 'yellow wavy-coated retriever' was or looked like. Nous might have been a yellow sport from a litter of black pups when St John's water dogs (something like a lighter, less hairy Newfoundland) were crossed with a setter.

Certainly wavy-haired retrievers existed, and it does seem that there is an element of setter in them. We also know that Lord Tweedmouth crossed his retrievers at least once with a setter, and that resulted in offspring very like the modern golden. Certainly Nigel is in many ways more like a setter than a Labrador, although yellow Labradors and golden retrievers are often closely associated in the modern dog-owner's mind. Having owned both I can vouch for the fact that they are very different breeds.

As a result of Lord Tweedmouth's breeding programme, golden retrievers were first accepted by the Kennel Club as a show breed in 1903 as 'Flat Coats – Golden'. They were first shown five years later and recognised as a breed in 1911 as 'Retrievers (Golden and Yellow)'. Their popularity both as gundogs and with the pet-owning public was rapid, and by 1920 their name had changed and become officially recognised as 'Golden Retriever'.

Eighty-eight years later we arrive at the birth of Nigel – who, Lord Tweedmouth would be horrified to know – is completely gun-shy and cowers in a corner if a balloon pops.

Lord Tweedmouth's breeding programme certainly did not cater for Nigel's extreme fear of bangs that makes him completely useless as a gundog – although that only becomes a problem once a year on bonfire night – but the genetic disposition to fetching a thrown object from a muddy, awkward, wet place and bringing it triumphantly back is right at the core of his being. As is the timing of the subsequent shake so that it drenches and spatters the owner.

He does adore fetching things from water, and here at Longmeadow we often have plenty of water to go fetching in.

For a start there is the river Arrow, running just a hundred yards from the back door, and another stream parallel to the garden that flows into it. But much more exciting are the floods that often appear, sometimes in a matter of an hour on an otherwise dry day, as water rushes down from the mountains in mid-Wales and spills out on to the Herefordshire flood plain.

When the ground is saturated – which at Longmeadow can be for months on end in a wet winter, and most winters here are very wet – the water meadows surrounding us become a flooded plain, making a lake about half a mile wide and a couple of miles long. Although very wet, it is also very beautiful, and no one appreciates it more than Nigel.

What is not so beautiful is the slow process of the ground soaking up all this water, creating fields slick with mud and vast puddles the size of large garden ponds, though too shallow to swim in. But this does not seem to diminish Nigel's pleasure as he sploshes around happily.

But in summer heavy rain further up the river in the Welsh

hills, especially after a very dry spell, will send the water spilling over the river and streams so that it sits on the hard ground for a day or so, often under a completely dry blue sky, and then will disappear almost overnight as it soaks into the soil. These are the floods that Nigel loves to swim in, striking out across fields in a half swimming, half paddling fashion as the water levels rise and fall with the ground. I have often started splashing out with him to suddenly find the water up to my waist as the ground, which appears so flat when grassy, reveals all its dips and hollows. This is when he is at his happiest: wet, chasing sticks and swimming along with them in his mouth, a water dog through and through.

We often walk in the Black Mountains and, when we come to any stream, Nigel will always find the deepest part and lie down in it, submerging himself as much as possible to cool off. If he cannot find a stream then a puddle will serve as well, the muddier the better.

For all its beautiful colour, Nigel's coat has a coarse outer layer that lies flat against his body. This makes it exceptionally good at repelling water. He can be dripping wet when he comes out, shake a couple of times and be miraculously dry in seconds. As he invariably comes indoors and stretches out when still sopping wet, it is just as well we have stone floors in the house. Underneath that is a second, much softer coat that keeps him warm and, because it is fairly oily, also resists water, so it rarely gets truly soaked. But when it does it is always a shock to see how lean and slim Nigel's body is – which is why he was able to jump with such ease before he hurt himself (although even now, injured and getting old, he can still leap incredibly well).

The feathering along the back of his legs and on his tummy and tail – especially his tail – may not add much to his water resistance or heat but, flying behind him like a pennant, it is a huge part of his – and all golden retrievers' – beauty.

13. Happy

Nigel smiles a lot. Not the crinkly, toothy, squinty-eyed grin that some dogs produce when they see you – which, adorable as it can be, is not really a smile at all but a pleasurable submissive gesture and almost invariably accompanied by tail wagging and some side to side movement – but the relaxed, slack-mouthed beam of someone pleased with their lot. This has nothing to do with other dogs or people, but often has a lot to do with a stick or ball that he has been playing with and is now between his front paws ready for the next match of fun. Life at that point is very, very good. So Nigel beams, the corners of his

A studio portrait of my father's
golden retriever, Barney,
taken around 1946. He looks
remarkably like Nell.

Meg was my grandmother's corgi and
my first memories of her were as an
old, irritable dog I was rather wary of.
But this portrait, taken some years
before I was born, shows her to
be a lovely little dog.

My twin sister
Alison and me
aged two in 1957.
Meg looks on
disapprovingly.

Gretel, aged about 10 weeks, chewing our black Labrador Sam.
The tolerance of older dogs towards puppies always amazes me.
Note the parched grass of that long hot summer.

Our first house in Ufton Road, London N1, was chosen as much for the size
of the garden for Gretel to play in as any considerations of the house.

Gretel and I watching gannets in the
Outer Hebrides, summer 1983.

Eric was our first terrier. Like all good terriers he was more than half mad, bad tempered and a wonderful character. This was his special bed.

Gretel and Eric just before Gretel died. We always took our dogs to work with us in our London jewellery days.

Posing with a long-suffering terrier as scarf. Outer Hebrides, 1983.

Baffin and Beaufort would play until exhausted and then fall asleep, often with Beaufort lying right on top of his big brother.

We took a week's holiday in a cottage in Wales in summer 1986 with four dogs and a two-month-old baby. It seemed to rain all the time but there was obviously a gap in which to light my pipe...

Whilst out on a boat on Loch Hourne on the west coast of Scotland in summer 1991 we were delivered a telegram telling us our bid for Longmeadow had been accepted.

Beaufort was happiest in or near water and swam fearlessly.

Poppy the Jack Russell was Eric's posthumous
daughter, and as gentle as he was truculent.

Red. She was hopeless at everything except for carrying two tennis balls in her
mouth and being completely lovable. That was more than enough.

Taken about 1997 at Longmeadow. Red was Beaufort's niece and her arrival gave him a fresh lease of life. Poppy, as usual, is sitting on Red's tail.

No dog ever loved a cuddle more than Red. My birthday, Longmeadow, 2002

All our dogs have loved to swim in the river and then flop onto the stone floors of the house, leaving their damp shadow.

mouth high, his tongue out, his eyes soft and shining and his tail wagging.

At times like this he radiates goodwill and simple pleasure, which has the desired effect of provoking greater happiness in me by playing with him. I feel happier seeing him; he feels tremendously happy – we are all thoroughly cheered up.

I think that this is an important reason why we love our dogs. We get visible and straightforward feedback from them when we do something to please them. There are no strings attached, no complications or trade-offs, no debts accruing or owing, no judgement of any kind made. You throw a ball or scratch an ear and the dog likes it and lets you know. That is it. Get to know that dog – usually yours, with whom you build an intimate and close relationship – and there is a pattern and history of this. Both of you recognise it and seek it out. It makes both your worlds a better place. Dogs' brains get flooded with dopamine and serotonin just as humans' do. Happiness rewards us by triggering not just momentary pleasure but also a sense of more lasting well-being. Happiness is contagious, and happy dogs make for happier owners and vice versa. When our dogs wriggle with evident pleasure at seeing us, we instantly feel better about ourselves and the world. We are made happier by their happiness.

The other side of that coin is that anxious, angry people are much more likely to have badly behaved, potentially dangerous dogs, although that cycle can be broken by a good dog imbuing its owner with a sense of calm and wellbeing. And if you have an anxious, unhappy dog, the best possible thing for it is to be calm, consistent and reassuring, as well as responding to signs of its own pleasure with playfulness. Both dog and man can make each other better.

Because many dog owners share a rich and fulfilling emotional life with their dogs, often just as rich and fulfilling as any they have with other humans, it is easy to anthropomorphise and project on to them thought processes that they just do not have. I always feel deeply uncomfortable when owners talk about their pets as though they were human, because this seems to diminish the relationship rather than enhance it. I often look at Nigel sleeping in front of the fire and think what an extraordinary thing it is to have this large animal sharing the house and how dependent that relationship is upon him choosing to go along with it rather than me enforcing it. This seems to me much more mysterious and wonderful than acting as though he is a four-footed human.

No dog has a moral code or feels guilt or rationalises our absences, knows what we are doing when we are not with them or indeed can override any of the instinctive canine triggers.

Dogs can learn behavioural tricks that please us because they fit in with the human idea of behaviour, and if they are to share our houses some of these – like not jumping on to furniture when wet and dirty, or not pooing at random around the house – are necessary, even though tricks they remain. But the shared emotions are real and meaningful, albeit expressed in different ways and for different reasons, and bind us across species rather than subjugating dogs into quasi little humanoids.

Mind you, Nigel's happiness is not always of the beaming, tail-wagging, extrovert kind. While going for a walk, having his dinner, or preparing to chase a ball are all guaranteed to make him very happy indeed, so is lying on the sofa with his head on a cushion.

14. Luxury

Nigel's love of luxury – which he has been working on with great focus since an early age – has become almost fetishistic in his advanced years.

A pillow is good but two so much better. His own bed can be very comfy but a sofa or a human bed does the job with just that little bit of extra effect – and no dog has ever taken more pleasure in maximum comfort than Nigel. He stretches out, head raised at the perfect elevation on a pillow, his body so relaxed that it almost flows into the softness of the mattress, moaning gently with pleasure. As well he might.

He also likes to sit on my lap when I am in an armchair

by the fire and will climb up in a manner that I suspect he regards as stealthy but is in fact just insistent. Once balanced on my knees he settles himself with much huffing and puffing, turning and squirming until properly comfy and then sinks into a deep and heavy-limbed sleep that leaves me quite unable to read my book or watch the screen, let alone reach for the glass that is tantalisingly close to hand – were it not for seventy pounds of Nigel pinioning me to the chair.

And although all experience is that letting a dog up on to the furniture – let alone a bed – is the thin end of a very dodgy wedge with the inevitable consequence of a filthy wet animal leaping up on clean covers or becoming possessive and truculent when told to move, in practice I think that this is something that can be negotiated. If it suits you to have the dogs on or in bed then it suits the dog too. Everyone is happy.

But as in all things to do with one's pets, it is important to be consistent. You cannot blame a muddy dog for leaping on to a favourite chair just after it has been cleaned when it was encouraged to do exactly the same a few days earlier when the chair was dirty and the dog was clean. It helps to have an old jacket that you can put anywhere for the dog to lie on that can be put in the washing machine if it becomes too sordid. I used to have an old tweed jacket that Gretel slept on in the car or whenever we travelled and it made her feel immediately at home wherever we were. It will smell comfortingly of you and be familiar – as well as protecting a much cleaner surface beneath it if need be. But I never got round to doing this with Nigel and now it is too late. His fastidiousness demands silks and satins, the softest down duvets, cashmere or alpaca rather than a tatty old bit of tweed.

He is a lost cause. Ruined.

15. The Box Balls

There are two doors out of the back yard: one leads to the Spring Garden, and the other takes a path dividing the old herb beds, through the box balls and into the greenhouse yard.

The box balls are much more important to us in real life than they are to the television garden. Television needs transformation – ideally with that dreadful word 'jeopardy' involved. Other than box blight, which of course excited everyone very much because of the possible drama attached, the box balls do not '*do*' anything at all. But they '*be*' very well indeed.

There are sixty-four of them, all different but all roughly the same size and shape. Although we call them the 'balls', there has never been any attempt to make them spherical. They are cobbles, and each one is cut according to my whim and intuitive fancy at the time. We had brought about ten of the box plants from London – which makes them almost forty years old now – and they were all cones. None was spherical. I cut the tops of the cones and gradually the rest responded to clipping to become roughly round. But the rest were a ragbag of scrawny hedging plants and cuttings and the final twenty or so were tiny when I planted them. I try not to think about how to do it but just let the blades flow. Other than the strain on one's back it is not hard. There is no stress (no jeopardy) attached. It takes between eight and sixteen hours to cut them and clear it up and I normally do it over a few days, never doing fewer than eight at a time so there is a rhythm.

I had no intention of planting box there of any shape. I intended to make borders, but as I dug it quickly became apparent that this was a cobbled yard and the cobbles were laid over stone. There was almost no soil at all. So I dug the planting holes and kept the cobbles, which I used to lay around the box. Part of the problem now is that they have exhausted their planting holes, and the roots are growing into rocky subsoil so are weak and stressed and therefore more susceptible to attack by the box blight fungus.

But from the outset the rhythm was pleasing. This is a much underrated thing in a garden. Simple repeated shapes always look good. The uniformity of colour is easy on the eye and – as is so often the case – the spaces between the solid objects were as interesting as the objects themselves.

I write in an old hop kiln looking down on them, and walk through them every time I go to the greenhouse – which is perhaps ten times a day. That makes nigh on a hundred thousand times. I have cut them about twenty-five times. They are old friends.

But friends that are in a poor way. They are suffering. We are spraying them weekly with seaweed and are trying Biochar sprinkled round the roots – both of which are designed to boost their defence systems so the new growth will resist the fungus.

But perhaps they will have to be grubbed out. It will be an opportunity – telly would love it . . . Drama! Jeopardy! I can see an interviewer asking me how I *feel*. The answer is I would feel sad because in many ways they are the hub of the garden.

All of this is lost on our Nigel. It washes over and above him. These are not cares that can be shared with a dog.

But I associate Nigel with a certain happy gait whenever he goes through the box balls. His step rises to a stiff-legged, joyous prance. His tail becomes a hoisted, wafting pennant.

Going through them towards the greenhouse means that he is off on a jaunt. The greenhouse yard is where any TV crews or gardeners might be found to bark a greeting at and have larks. He has always been a party boy.

Nigel has seen the box balls waste and fade from sixty-four solid, lustrous green bobbles, each one the size of a boulder, to the threadbare, worn-out travesties they have become. The fact that he invariably stops and cocks his leg against at least one is not what is responsible for their demise; it is the predations of box blight, which has ripped through the garden. Nigel doesn't care. As long as he can shimmy in between them, recovering errant balls and occasionally rooting out a mouse, then they are doing their job just fine.

In summer the space between each ball is filled with a yellow foam of corydalis, stopping him shimmying between them and scratching his shanks in an easeful way. The corydalis looks better than the box nowadays, but was self-sown and unintended and has probably done little to stop the spread of the fungus causing the blight by restricting the airflow. No matter. That battle is all but lost.

16. The Englishman and His Dogs

Although some of us take it for granted that we love our dogs and that they are part of our families, it has not always been so. The view of dogs as scavengers, little better than vermin, is still to be found in large parts of the East today, and was transmitted to the West via the Bible. This was the prevalent attitude in the UK that lasted well into the seventeenth century. Throughout the Elizabethan period, dogs were regarded as unclean, filthy, promiscuous and gluttonous. 'Dog' was always a term of contempt.

A hound, on the other hand, was always seen as a noble, valiant animal. Since the late fourteenth century, hunting or game dogs were only permitted to people above a certain social level. So greyhounds, hounds and spaniels were regarded as gentlemen's dogs and reflected their owner's virtues commensurate with their rank.

Nevertheless, despite covering the great sweep of humanity with more insight and perception than any other author, there is barely a single canine companion or pet mentioned in the whole of Shakespeare's work. Dogs were beginning to be openly praised – but only up to a point.

The truth was that dogs reflected the status of their owners. Well-born people had dogs that were regarded with affection. The low-born had curs and mongrels.

By the middle of the seventeenth century, dogs were generally acknowledged as man's best friend. This was a complete volte-face from just a century earlier and there were plenty of public pronouncements disagreeing or reinterpreting the Bible's attitude towards dogs.

The lap dog became ubiquitous in the sixteenth century, especially among wealthy ladies. This was most often a toy spaniel in the sixteenth century and a pug in the seventeenth and eighteenth. Other than pugs, Chinese dogs – such as Pekinese, shih-tzu – did not become popular till the nineteenth century. Anne Boleyn was devoted to her pet dog and this was typical of ladies of the court. Mary Queen of Scots took her little dog to the block and it was extricated from under the skirts of her headless body, soaked in its mistress's blood.

In seventeenth-century engravings of Oxford and Cambridge there are dogs everywhere. Most people kept them, not least for protection of their houses at night. Mastiffs were the universal guard dog, muzzled during the day and left to roam free at night. Greyhounds and spaniels were always acceptable gifts among the aristocracy, and gentry loved their hounds with a passion; they were often fed and housed better than servants.

In all great houses greyhounds, terriers and spaniels roamed unfettered with accompanying 'nastiness – bones and turds littering the hall'. Forecourts in front of houses became dog-free zones to keep them clean to receive visitors.

Many seventeenth-century dogs still had practical functions. They pulled sledges, and carts – even ploughs. Shepherds, drovers, butchers all invariably used them as a tool of their trade. In big houses with a busy kitchen they were used to turn the spit in a wheel. But most working dogs were regarded unsentimentally and were hanged or drowned when they no longer served a purpose. 'My old dog Quorn was killed and baked for his grease of which he yielded 11 lbs,' wrote a Dorset farmer in 1698, with the 'my old dog Quorn' touched with affection despite his grizzly rendering.

(Hanging a dog seems appallingly barbaric to us, but when you consider how many people were hanged in that era for what we now consider minor offences, perhaps it is not so odd; given that there were no injections or bullets to do the job, it was a noose, a knife or drowning.)

James I had his favourite hounds Jowler and Jewell – although Jewell was shot by James's wife Anne when she mistook it for a deer. Indeed, James was accused of loving his dogs more than his subjects – a charge laid at the door of many a father and husband since.

Perhaps influenced by his exile spent with the French court, his grandson Charles II was obsessed with his spaniels, which developed from the toy spaniels of the Tudor court. But they went out of favour with the arrival of William and Mary, who favoured pugs, which remained popular lap dogs throughout the eighteenth century. The two were combined when the toy spaniel was crossed with the pug to give the modern King Charles spaniel with the short, compressed nose.

It seems that the word 'pet' to describe an animal kept solely for the pleasure of its company as a member of the family did not really come into play until the late seventeenth century, and was taken from the usage of 'pet' to describe someone, usually a child, who was spoilt and indulged. Charles II's spaniels epitomised this perception as pets being essentially lap dogs that were indulged in a pampered and somehow immoral, if charming, fashion.

Throughout the eighteenth century, pet dogs were increasingly common and accepted, but largely the preserve of aristocracy and the newly wealthy, and in particular of women who kept small dogs as useless and indulgent adornments to an increasingly pampered and frivolous lifestyle. These were dogs as fashion accessories rather than the essential working colleagues or aides in manly pursuits like hunting, which had characterised them in previous centuries.

In 1796 a dog tax was introduced – along with a huge raft of other taxes to raise money to fight the Napoleonic wars; it was noted at this time that there were over a million dogs in the country, and most were pets rather than working dogs. Pets increased as towns did – mainly because the need for a working dog was far less in towns than the countryside. So the dog as a member of the family rather than part of the tools of the trade or one of the farm animals became the norm.

As society became – and becomes – increasingly urban, pets have become increasingly important within that family unit. One of the ironies of modern life is that the less contact we have with uncontrolled nature, the more we want pets.

Pets follow certain definitions. The first is that they are allowed into the house. In the past they were also allowed –

97

and often taken – into church; almost every parish church had a dog-whipper, whose job was to remove ill-disciplined dogs from the building. One of the main purposes of the communion rails was to keep dogs away from the altar.

The second is that they are given individual names. By the eighteenth century it became common to give a litter of hounds names beginning with the same initial. There were occasional incidences of human names being given to dogs from medieval times, but this became much more common and indeed standard by the middle of the eighteenth century, and was indicative of the close personal bond between pet and owner. This was a particularly British thing: in France, for example, dogs have rarely been given Christian names. Call your dog Nigel rather than Nautilus or Nibbler and you are making him part of the family rather than just a possession. Names always confer status.

They also go a long way to prevent an animal from being cooked and eaten. The principle is that we cannot eat any creature that has a name and that we know as part of our family. Certainly when raising farm animals destined for the table, it is an absolute rule not to give them names. Hence our horror at certain Asian countries raising dogs for their meat. This is not a case of revulsion at cruelty to animals but of crossing a family line. It is too close to eating one of us.

The assimilation of pets into families became marked by portraiture – especially in the grander families. Favourite dogs had appeared in royal portraits from Tudor times, and in 1637 Van Dyck painted Charles I's five eldest children with an enormous mastiff in their midst.

In the eighteenth century dogs increasingly featured in portraiture, and the death of favoured dogs began to be marked by memorials – often expensive and ornate, such as the memorial to 'RINGWOOD, AN OTTER-HOUND of extraordinary Sagacity' that is built into a water feature in the peerless garden at Rousham in Oxfordshire, designed by William Kent for General Dormer in the late 1730s.

Hounds were always particularly loved because they were a way in which otherwise emotionally inarticulate men could love and be loved, without embarrassment, and without stepping outside the codes of behaviour of their class and time. However absurd or socially strange that world may be to us now, the emotions were real and recognisable. Their faithfulness was invariably commemorated, and real grief and sense of loss expressed. Dogs had shifted from being either as indulged lap dogs, or tools of the trade to be brutally dispatched when no longer serviceable, to being friends, companions and beloved intimates.

I remember reading T. H. White's *The Sword in the Stone* when I was a boy, and being profoundly moved by the passage when the book's hero, Wart, who is to become King Arthur, watches as the favourite hound of the king's huntsman, Master Twyti, is mortally wounded by the boar they are chasing, and has to be killed by Robin Wood's curved sword or falchion. White exactly catches the stoicism and depths of anguish that any dog owner who has to take a pet to be destroyed knows far too well.

'Master Twyti drew one leg slowly from under the boar, stood up, took hold of his knee with his right hand, moved it enquiringly in various directions, nodded to himself and stretched his back straight. Then he picked up his spear without saying anything and limped over to Beaumont. He knelt down beside him and took his head on his lap. He stroked Beaumont's head and said, "Hark to Beaumont. Softly, Beaumont, mon amy. Oyez a Beaumont the Valiant. Swef, le douce Beaumont, swef, swef." Beaumont licked his hand but could not wag his tail. The huntsman nodded to Robin, who was standing behind, and held the hound's eyes with his own. He said, "Good dog, Beaumont the valiant, sleep now, old friend Beaumont, good old dog." Then Robin's falchion let Beaumont out of this world, to run free with Orion and roll among the stars.

'The Wart did not like to watch Master Twyti for a moment or two. The strange little leathery man stood up without saying anything and whipped the hounds off the corpse of the boar as he was accustomed to do. He put his horn to his lips and blew the four long notes of the mort without a quaver. But he was blowing the notes for a different reason, and he startled the Wart because he seemed to be crying.'

The pet dog as an integral part of the family took until the middle of the nineteenth century to become accepted and established – inspired, as was so much in Victorian life, by the way that Victoria and Albert included portraits of their dogs alongside their children as part of the royal family. Dickens portrayed dogs as emblematic of a loving and balanced home, and we have moving records of Charles Darwin's dogs being at the centre of an otherwise emotionally deprived childhood; they remained essential members of his large family.

Also, as industrialisation meant that more and more people were forced to live in towns to find work, the keeping of a dog was a nostalgic remnant of the lost connection with the natural and agrarian world. You might not need a sheepdog in the backstreets of a cotton town, but a dog of sorts was part of the lost life that was shared within living memory. Close contact with a pet bred a sense of morality in the treatment of animals and the rise of animal welfare in husbandry.

The idea of dogs as curs was much influenced by packs of stray dogs, and during plague years in Elizabethan and Jacobean London they were rounded up and killed as it was thought that they spread the pestilence. Those that killed them were paid a penny a carcass. I remember the horror of seeing mountains of cattle and sheep corpses slowly and ineffectually being burnt during the foot and mouth epidemic of 2002, and how eerily silent the countryside was, stripped of the lowing and bleating of animals. How much worse to see dogs piled up in the streets of Jacobean London!

It was not until the middle of the Victorian period that the notion of a 'stray' dog became unacceptable, with their rightful and proper place being within a loving household. One of the ironies of this was that the establishment of rescue services such as Battersea Dogs Home, ostensibly to reunite lost family pets with their owners, was also to rid the streets of unseemly and unowned mongrels.

Pets were, above all, respectable and proper. Still today the sight of a mongrel attached by a lead to a homeless person, as loved and loving as any pampered pet or working dog, both living on the street, is a moving reminder of the domestic morality of Victorian life.

17. Training

Nigel has never been clever. He is not a scholarship boy. But when he was six months old I decided it was time to begin some serious training over and above basic obedience. He clearly liked learning and would sit, heel, and pretty much come when called. He was ready for the next stage.

In fact golden retrievers are apparently rated as one of the brightest of all breeds, but that is based upon the speed with which they can acquire instruction – and Nigel has always been astonishingly easy to train. But training tends to develop the instincts that a particular breed has been selected for; in other words, harness what they want to do anyway. We have a sheepdog, Meg, who works large flocks of sheep with astonishing skill and control. But when you throw a ball for her she ignores the ball and tries to round up Nigel, who will have inevitably gone and retrieved it. On the other hand, he's not so hot on sheep wrangling . . .

Every gene in Nigel's makeup strains to go and find things and bring them back. Life is always better for him with something in his mouth, but best of all if he has gone and got it. To love him properly you have to celebrate and relish those retrieving abilities.

Most dog owners value the working heritage and abilities of popular breeds like spaniels, retrievers, Labradors, terriers, setters, pointers, etc., yet never work them, so rarely train them beyond basic obedience. But I think that dogs with very specific abilities tend to be happier and more fulfilled if those traits are developed and exercised regularly. A spaniel may never hear the sound of gunshot but, over and above racing after a ball or stick, will be blissfully happy finding a thrown lure in a park and returning it to its owner in a controlled and disciplined fashion.

What this comes down to is that all training is a matter of giving your dog the right signals at the right time. The hard part is to teach them to override distractions, be it another dog, extreme noise, or a ball suddenly bouncing across their path. In essence those are the moments when they are waiting for the next signal from you to the exclusion of all other signals. When you train any dog to have a little bit of obedience, it is a matter of curbing its natural tendencies and trying to control it, mostly to make the owner's life a little easier. It is a matter of restraint and even domination. Though to try and bully the dog into craven submission is doomed to failure, however much it makes you feel leader of your pack. Dogs always work best with you, not for you.

But training a dog to work at what it instinctively wants to do and does well is never one-sided. It brings owner and dog together in learning and mastering something. It is more than just a matter of making the dog do what you want, when and how you want it. Both parties are complicit in this performance. The dog is not working for you so much as with you. You become a team, dependent upon each other. This is deeply satisfying. Any owner quickly discovers that every working dog loves working above all else, so not only is it fascinating to share that working experience, but also they will love you all the more keenly as a result. Everybody wins.

When I decided to step up Nigel's training, I thought back to 1976 and the advice given to me in the pub by the keeper Mr Brown, and I trained Nigel as I had trained my Labrador Gretel all those years ago. The Keeper might have terrorised our childhood walks with our dogs in Hampshire, but he always had a couple of spaniels at his heels and they were noticeably calm and obedient; by all accounts, no dogs were better retrievers than those trained by him.

The first thing with any dog, Mr Brown said, was always to feed it in a disciplined manner. Make him sit before giving him his food and wait for the command to start eating. Once he instinctively does this, occasionally take the food away from him in mid-meal, make him sit, wait, and continue eating again only when instructed. When he does this reliably he should – eventually – do almost anything.

His second rule was that I should not attempt any gundog training beyond very simple commands such as 'Come', 'Sit' and 'Stay' until any dog was six months old. When the dog was ready – and every dog was different he said, with a good Labrador being ready for work at five–six months compared to many golden retrievers which were hopeless until over twelve months – I should progress to very short ten-minute training sessions following twenty minutes of walking and playing. The key was to get him to concentrate solely on my instructions for that ten-minute period. It meant complete concentration and I had to work at it as hard as him. When he could do ten minutes well and was maintaining that concentration right to the end, I should extend it to fifteen minutes and finally twenty. That was plenty long enough.

Once the dog had let off steam and run around for fifteen

minutes or so, I should call him and make him sit and stay by me – and he would only be ready to begin working on training if he could do both those things reliably. I should start by making him walk at heel on a lead. 'Do not yank or force him into this' he said. 'Start slowly and be firm but gentle. Everything should be geared to making the dog want to please you rather than subjugating it to your will.'

He also said never hit a dog. The worst he did was to take his cap off – and in the ten years or so I had known him I had never seen him out of doors without his tweed flat cap – and flick it lightly at the dog's head. After a couple of times just reaching for his cap was enough. 'Reward is the key,' he said, 'not punishment. The dog wants to please you more than anything else. Tell him he has done well. He will respond to the tone of your voice. But also carry some bits of biscuit or cheese (all dogs love cheese) in your pocket and give him a scrap when he does exactly what you command. By the same token never reward him if he only half does the job.'

'Always use exactly the same commands,' he went on. '"Here" is different to "Come here". Keep it simple and keep it consistent. Just his name and the command.'

He told me that the secret was to be completely focused on the process myself, and not to let the dog be distracted or to play or do anything that I had not commanded. At first this would be really hard. For a young dog it is the concentration that is as difficult as actually mastering the commands.

'Get him to sit and wait by your side. Then throw the lure.'

I was not sure what a lure was.

Mr Brown tried to hide his disdain at my ignorance. 'Something soft but heavy enough to throw a distance,' he explained. 'We always use a small stuffed canvas bag with a couple of partridge wings stitched to it so the dog gets used to carrying feathers.'

Poor Nigel had a downgraded version of this made up of one of my old socks with a heavy, solid rubber ball inside, but you can buy fancy canvas-covered versions.

'Get the dog to retrieve the lure and bring it back,' Mr Brown said. 'Be patient. Concentrate. Even if it is frustratingly unsuccessful, don't get cross and don't carry on for more than ten minutes. Just put the lure away and carry on walking.

'Never mix work and play. Only use the lure for training. Treat it as a tool not a toy. When you produce it, the dog will soon pick up the signals that it is time for work and automatically be as eager as it is when waiting to be fed, and should be poised and completely alert for your command.'

He finished his pint.

'It is easy to get a retriever to retrieve,' he said. 'The hard bit is to get them to bring it right back to your hand. Most will stop short, until you walk up to them so it can be thrown again. The last few yards are just as important as all the others put together. Unless he brings it back to your hand and gives it when you ask for it then the job is not done. Don't worry about how far you throw it or where it goes until he can bring it right back to you every time.'

'Another?' I said.

'Go on then,' he replied. 'A quick one.' It was the nearest we got to intimacy and both of us knew the battle lines would be redrawn as soon as we got back out to the woods and fields.

'In the end it is simple enough,' he said. 'Train the dog to wait, sitting, until you are ready for it to go. You don't have to train it to find or retrieve – it will do that anyway. But train it to bring the retrieved object to you straight away and train it to bring it right to your hand and only release it when you ask for it – but do so immediately. Then train it to sit or walk quietly by your side until asked to go again.'

Mr Brown finished his drink, wiped his mouth with the back of a surprisingly fine-boned hand and pulled his cap from a pocket. 'If everyone took the trouble to train their dogs properly then it would save them – and us – a lot of trouble.'

That was the last and only time I ever spoke to him, but I remembered every word when it came to training Nigel. I wonder what he would have thought if he'd known that his advice had indeed made Nigel very biddable – but that rather than fetching pheasants from ditches, he had instead become a star of the small screen.

18. The Cottage Garden

The garden has three main paths running down its length, the central one bisecting the whole plot. Call Nigel from one end and the chances are that he will appear at some point along its length from one side or other, rounding the corner at a gallop and funnelling down to you before screeching to a slightly unsuccessful halt.

If he is not using the paths like the lanes on a racetrack, he will lie across them, effectively blocking them in order not to miss any action that might prove to be interesting, but at the same time avoiding having to go and look for it. Anything that comes to anybody in the garden at

Longmeadow comes via one of the three main paths.

The central path runs like a nave down the garden, starting at right angles to the centre of the Lime Walk. It runs through the Cottage Garden flanked by chunky box hedges and espalier pears. I bought the hedge from someone's garden over twenty years ago. The advert in the paper said that there were 'good-sized box plants for sale' but forgot to mention that these plants were forming a good-sized hedge between the vendor and her neighbour!

These were the only box hedges in the garden for a while, but every year I took cuttings and gradually accumulated hundreds of young plants that eventually edged most of the borders and paths in the garden. To Nigel all these hedges – about a mile of them at their fullest extent – exist only as a surface of ideal height, a kind of green, living shelf, to place a ball on in order that it might be thrown. Box blight has ravaged them all and many have been grubbed out, but hundreds of yards remain and, like the box balls, they are being treated with a weekly feed of seaweed and now Biochar in an effort to make them fight off the fungal disease.

The Cottage Garden, conveniently near the kitchen, was for many years the main vegetable plot, but is now filled with roses and herbaceous perennials mainly in soft, pastel colours. It is subdivided into twenty-two different beds bounded by mature box hedges. The whole space is bounded by hornbeam hedges beneath pleached limes. It is very structured and symmetrical with – I hope – a careless abundance and abandon of planting, and altogether a far cry from the open area of rough grass that was first ripped open by a huge tractor and plough on a spring evening in 1993.

So pinks, lemon yellows, lavenders, mauves, pale blues and whites dominate the colour palette, although the true higgledy-piggledy spirit of a cottage garden knows no such self-consciousness, and in practice these are flowers that we love and yet have no home within the tight restrictions of the Jewel Garden. Phlox, foxgloves, aquilegias, nepeta, forget-me-nots, hollyhocks and lupins share the beds with fruit bushes, ornamental kale, and edgings that might as easily be parsley or pinks. Clematis and sweet peas climb wigwams made from bean sticks cut from the coppice, and there are more than forty different kinds of shrub roses, most still small but in a year or two they will all be substantial shrubs. As I write this I realise that the Cottage Garden is becoming a rose garden with added texture. So be it. You can never have too many roses.

As well as the structure made by flowering shrubs and perennials, annuals and biennials of all kinds are terribly important for this kind of gardening. Hardy annuals are ideal because they can be sown directly, avoiding all the expense of raising seedlings under cover. Marigolds and poppies, nigella, alyssum, cornflowers, larkspur and lavatera all weave among the more permanent planting of the Cottage Garden.

Eight tall fastigiate Irish yews are in the centre of the small square borders, and have now grown from the original three-foot plants we bought in 1995, via various shiftings around in the garden trying to find the right home for them, to substantial columnar trees that would now be too big to move. Although as recently as spring 2008, Sarah and I walked them round from the walled garden, so they have doubled in size in the past eight years.

And yew serves to create a monument to Nigel. In one corner, by the entrance from the cold frames, a topiary Nigel, made from two yew bushes that were left over from the yew hedges I planted at the end of the Jewel Garden, is taking form. It is being trained and clipped around the most basic of bamboo structures, consisting of a cross-strut for his back and a couple of uprights for his legs. For the first couple of years this was greeted with hilarity and condescension by the *Gardeners' World* team, all very polite of course, but they certainly did not see the dog within the growing green form. But after three years it is now becoming canine, if not exactly a portrait. Refinement can come later. Nevertheless Nigel it is, although he is short of a front leg so that has been quietly planted and will catch up with the rest of his body.

Nigel is yet to acknowledge this tribute to him and marches

past it with never so much as a sideways glance. Acclaim has made him haughty. I admit it is a bit larger than life-size, somewhat greener and a bit fuzzy round the edges, but it is him all right, growing quietly in the garden.

19. Telly

Nigel crept into television bit by bit. It was never my plan to use him on screen; he simply did what he always does and followed me round the garden, bringing me balls to throw or waiting on standby for balls that might be thrown. Gradually more and more shots included him, although sometimes I think it was a deliberate ploy of his, slowly insinuating himself into every scene until he became indispensable, edging me aside to become his straight man, a walk-on to feed him the best lines.

They say that certain film stars 'stick to the lens' – always being the most interesting, attractive thing in a shot, regardless of what they or anyone else is doing or saying. Nigel is just like that. He is a terrible scene-stealer, with an uncanny ability to strike exactly the right pose that will look best on camera in any given circumstance.

Here is one example, plucked at random from scores like it. We were filming *Gardeners' World* at Longmeadow as usual, working through a very busy schedule that involved about eight different set-ups plus perhaps a dozen linking shots. Each set-up takes about an hour or so, so there is not much slack in the working day, and the director orchestrates things, moving the production team like chess pieces. As well as the director there might well be a producer, an assistant producer logging every shot, a runner or two, at least two and sometimes three cameramen, and a sound recordist. Just moving and positioning this travelling circus with their cameras, monitors and cables involves ingenuity and patience.

On this occasion, we all finally got into the desired positions and the director checked if I was ready.

'OK – Monty, just come round the corner with the barrow, pick up the pot, say your stuff to camera A, put the pot in the barrow and throw to camera B.'

'No problem,' I say. 'Standing by.'

'OK. Action!'

So I set off, pushing the barrow, and as I came round the

corner I heard one of the cameramen say, 'Hang on – just a mo' . . . the sunlight's just perfect . . . don't move . . . good boy – perfect.'

And as I came round the corner I saw Nigel lying exactly where I was to park the barrow, finding the one shaft of sunlight that had broken through the cloud all morning, his tail gently wafting like a preened, russet ostrich feather, filtering the light. He looked up and saw me – with I could swear, a slight smirk – and then demurely lowered his head on to his stretched-out paws.

The director called out the signal to end the scene: 'Cut!'

The sun went back in. Nigel shuffled off out of the way. Both camera-men congratulated themselves for capturing the magic moment and the director beckoned for me to do my required stuff now the star had completed his turn.

It happens time after time.

~

One of the reasons that we use Nigel so much is not just his innate ability to steal a scene but also his much more prosaic qualities. He very quickly learns simple things like when to come, where to walk and when to quietly lie down, and then can do these time after time without fluffing his lines. There is nothing that he does that a million other dogs couldn't do just as well, but very few of them would do them do so reliably, time after time, among the slightly chaotic, crowded circumstances of a telly shoot.

Although a television programme like *Gardeners' World* is carefully edited to appear as an easy, natural flow of action, the reality of filming is anything but that. Nowadays it takes a very focused ten-hour day to record something between fifteen and twenty minutes – and until recent tightening of budgets across all productions, it would take twice as long as that. When I started out in television nearly thirty years ago, to produce two to three minutes a day was perfectly acceptable, and more than five very unusual. Filming a practical magazine programme like *Gardeners' World* is much more like a drama than so-called 'reality' TV (which, in my experience, is not very real at all), with a script that has been through numerous drafts (although I rarely look at a script as, when I started doing television, I realised that I could never speak anyone else's lines like an actor. If I did not think it I could not say it. As a consequence I work out what I am going to talk about and then let the words look after themselves). The camera angles and positions will be carefully planned, using at least two and often three or even four separate cameras and a production team of about eight or nine people. Every action and every word will have to be repeated at least two or three times and often as many as seven or eight. I have often planted the same plant three or four times in the same spot or used up to three identical plants to keep them looking fresh. It is slow and painstaking and not at all like real life.

This can be tricky for the human in front of the cameras. What would otherwise be quite straightforward becomes either meaningless or impossible to memorise. Self-consciousness quickly kicks in and the essential absurdity of it all can inhibit the most straightforward of actions and comments. Without overstating the demands, it does require a mixture of concentration, suspension of disbelief and even some skill. And everyone who has done it will tell you that it is surprisingly tiring.

But Nigel has to do all this too, though without the talking. He too has to repeat every action half a dozen times at exactly the right moment – often with mind-numbingly slow minutes between takes when technical minutiae are discussed or problems fixed. Yet he does this with astonishing compliance, managing to hit markers time after time, even though in terms of common sense some of the things asked of him (and me) are perverse.

For example, Nigel and I will often have to walk from two points in the garden perhaps twenty yards apart and connected by a dead straight path that both of us go up and down all day long, but for the purposes of the shot take a completely circuitous route involving three or four completely unnecessary turns so that the camera can get maximum opportunity for 'passing shots' – i.e. glimpses of Nige and me crossing the line of the camera, often with suitable vegetation in the foreground. These passing shots have to be done because they are invaluable for editing purposes, helping to stitch together otherwise unconnected pieces of action without the viewer noticing any change of light, mood or geography.

The obvious and easiest way to get Nigel to do this is to have him walking to heel. This is not difficult and most well-trained dogs will trot along obediently just behind the owner. But then the director is likely to say 'That was great' (this is always followed by a 'but' and the request to do it again, better or simply different), 'but this time could Nigel go ahead of you and instead of turning left could you turn right at the first box hedge and then turn left by the carrots.'

Try getting a dog to distinguish between first and second left and a row of carrots and a bed of parsley. (In fact, try getting any non-gardener to do the same.)

The only way to make that work is to walk through with Nigel exactly where you want him to go, suppressing his instinct to go the route that we always take. Then to do it again – by which time the director will be fidgeting and saying very pointedly: 'Take your time, no problem, but we are all ready when you are . . .'

Then I point Nigel in the right direction and almost

invariably he does it dead right. Then he will do it again every time – dead right.

That is the real secret. Not just that he can be taught to do the necessary movements, but that he will repeat them as many times as necessary and wait patiently in between takes.

I do have a couple of incentives to help him. I always have a pocketful of small biscuits and occasionally reward him with a tiny morsel every time he gets something right. The danger of this is that he can become over-eager and simply fixate on my pocket rather than bounce along apparently full of the joys of spring.

The other even more potent weapon is to have a small yellow tennis ball in my pocket that, critically, has a squeak. So when asked if he could look in my direction while I am speaking rather than making eyes at the crew – Nigel is a terrible flirt – I will put the squeaky ball in my far pocket and give it a quick squeak just as the director says 'Action!' Nigel, terribly excited by this, then spends the rest of the take looking across to see where the noise and glorious hint of tennis ball aroma is coming from.

Occasionally we are asked to do things that are genuinely tricky. One day we had a jimmy jib – essentially a camera at the end of a thirty-foot pole that can rise and swoop from ground to aerial shot in one sweeping movement – and Nigel and I were asked to walk into the Cottage Garden looking jaunty and then look up and speak to this camera as it moved across and down from the sky. So, in due course we did as we were told.

'That was great . . . but this time could Nigel look up too?'

After three or four attempts we discovered that Nigel could not and would not look up too.

Then someone had the bright idea of tying a squeaky ring made of tennis ball material – clearly irresistible – to the jib so that it appeared above his head as it swooped down at us. This worked a treat and as I walk along and welcome you to that week's edition of *Gardeners' World*, Nigel stops and looks up with a smiling face at the camera, his ears pricked up, delighted not to see you but the lovely yellow ring thing attached to a length of garden twine and dangling from the camera.

This is not to say that he does not get bored. As a rule he likes a generous nap after his breakfast and in the normal course of events would regard a couple of hours' mid-morning sleep as the civilised thing to do. There are quite a few occasions on which filming is particularly slow, when it does appear that we are keeping him up, and in between takes he will stretch out and fall into a seemingly deep sleep in seconds, whereas if it is merely boredom he will lie with his head on his paws, weary but resigned to the absurdity of his master's strange profession.

20. The Long Walk

The Long Walk cuts across the garden as a narrow passageway and acts as a breathing space between the Cottage Garden and the Jewel Garden. It is also a very useful way to cut across the garden from the greenhouse yard to get down to the grass borders or Damp Garden or go up to the Mound and orchard.

It is simple but has had many incarnations in its time. Like the Lime Walk, which it lies parallel to, it is essentially an avenue of pleached limes crossed by two major paths going up the length of the garden and one smaller one linking the Damp Garden, grass borders and the Mound. This creates a series of narrow beds flanking the path. One of the reasons that the planting has changed is that as the hornbeam hedges that the limes are underplanted with have grown, so the shade has increased and their roots have become hungrier; thus anything growing beneath them has to compete hard for light, moisture and nutrients.

So, over the past twenty years we have used the walk for pumpkins, artichokes, giant alliums (fabulous, but they all rotted after flowering and with over a hundred bulbs at £5 a bulb it proved to be very costly bedding), sweet peas – which worked well with sixteen wigwams on either side so that it became a fragrant tunnel of flowers – but they did need watering a lot. Finally we planted a box hedge all the way down with what were intended to be topiary box balls spaced along the beds, underplanted with tulips in spring. The balls wouldn't play ball – it was a variety of box called 'Handsworthiensis' that is extremely robust but wants to grow upwards, and which reacted to being cut in the round by sulking. After a few years I let them become the cones that they always wanted to be.

This looked good – more than good, it looked great – but was the first place that box blight struck and we ripped out the hedging in 2014. I have left the topiary uncut for two years so they are shaggy and formless but are due for a trim soon.

Beneath them we have the wallflower 'Blood Red', daffodils and the tulip 'Ballerina' and *Acanthus spinosus*, which starts to get growing as the tulips die back, so it is a gaudy parade for a month or so and then a cool green corridor. The plan is to return it to the measured space that it was before, so that it acts as a launching point before leaping into the intensity of the Jewel Garden.

Nigel is always moving in the Long Walk, rarely looking left or right. It is a place to get to places, a route to somewhere else rather than a destination.

But little dogs like it and rootle about among the box and hedges, returning to the path before deviating off to the side again. We have always had little dogs as well as bigger ones; they are important members of our family, but they keep well out of the limelight. Always, that is, except Eric.

21. Eric

My mother did not really approve of Sarah and me setting up home together, partly because she thought, with some reason, that I was immature, feckless and impoverished, and partly perhaps because Sarah was already married to someone else. But neither factor deterred us, and after a couple of years that took us from Bristol to the North York Moors and a series of rented rooms in London, we moved into our house in De Beauvoir with its unusually large garden. This was ideal both for Sarah and me and Gretel – who had accompanied us on all our various travels.

As a house-warming present my mother gave Sarah a terrier

puppy called Eric. Sarah neither wanted nor needed a dog of any kind. Dogs were not really her thing. She had learned to love Gretel but she was in the package that came with me. If she had wanted a dog it would have been a lap dog, an adornment in the spirit of eighteenth-century ladies with their pugs. She certainly had no intention of becoming hitched to a half-demented terrier with a wonky leg and anger-management issues.

Eric was twelve weeks old and the only unsold pup from a large litter belonging to a farmer in Hampshire. He was half Jack Russell, half fox terrier. The result was either a leggy Jack Russell or a stunted fox terrier, depending on your view of the world, although this effect was modified by one of his forelegs being withered and a couple of inches shorter than the other, which accounted for the lack of any would-be owners. He also had terrible worms and mange, which meant that his fur was patchy with raw, scaly skin. He had never been inside a house and was almost wilfully un-housetrained (oh, the hours hanging around with a puppy in the rain as it sniffs every blade of grass, does nothing, finally comes indoors and pees on the carpet or poos over the crack in the floorboards . . .) and nervous of everything.

Other than that he was completely fine.

In fact Eric was more than fine. He was great, with an irrepressible character and huge personality. I like terriers of all kinds. They are fun and terrific companions.

Within a few weeks all the superficial physical problems were sorted out and the dodgy leg never slowed him down or bothered him in the least. Sarah, the most fastidious of people, grew to love him very much and, invariably, when he wasn't curled up with Gretel, it was her lap that he chose or an article of her clothing (usually the cleanest and most expensive) that he found to sleep on.

Every morning I would get up early and while Gretel trotted out into the dawn air, Eric would race up the three flights of stairs and leap into our bed to burrow down to lie at Sarah's feet. If ever I tried to extricate him before Sarah got up he bit me.

Eric had two great passions in life. One was to take on and fight any and every other male dog in the world, and the other was bricks. If a brick was not to hand then a stone would do and, failing that, the biggest, most awkward piece of wood he could find – but bricks were always best.

If I was gardening he would appear at my side with half a brick/stone/awkward bit of wood in his mouth and drop it in front of me. He would then hold both his legs together in front of him, one longer and twice as muscular as the other, and push and shove it in my path, stopping only to look up at me and bark piercingly. This would continue until I picked up said brick/stone/awkward bit of wood and threw it. You knew that the only way to stop the game was to ignore him.

But Eric would go on barking and prodding and badgering long after and beyond you were driven to distraction. So you duly gave in and threw and he would then madly chase and fetch it, twisting his body almost parallel to the ground to pick it up and bring it back to start the fun all over again. Every time you threw it he would always, always bring it back and repeat it all over again. All day.

I think he would have rather died than give up on the current trophy. One exceptional snowy and cold day in early May, Sarah and I walked across Haworth Moor to Top Withins, the inspiration for *Wuthering Heights*, situated on the bleak but beautiful hills above Huddersfield. Eric dragged a log at least twice the size and weight of himself through the snow and ice all the way there and regarded any attempt to take it from him as a tug of war. We ignored him in the hope that he would give up. When we finally reached the car, after a five-hour walk, he was so exhausted that he had to be lifted into the back, and spent the whole evening wrapped in a blanket being hand-fed restorative morsels with the log triumphantly by his side.

He hated all other male dogs with a kind of crazed vengeance. We learned to scan ahead on walks, checking the gender of other approaching dogs and slipping him on the lead before Eric got a whiff of testosterone. This was made complex because, despite his deep vein of inner rage and typically crazed terrier tenacity, Eric was not a particularly good fighter and often came off second best. On quite a few occasions he had to be whisked off to the vet to be stitched together again. Once he decided to attack a pair of particularly large Alsatians that dared to walk with a doggy swagger in his manor. In the ensuing fight, one bit through his head, puncturing his skull and slicing right down through his jaw. I rescued him, simultaneously apologising to the owner for failing to stop my dog making his suicide attack, and took him to the vet expecting a quick mercy injection to put him out of his misery. But a lot of stitches and a heavy dose of antibiotics later, and within a week he was back in fighting form, setting on a slavering Doberman with his usual sense of an appropriate opponent.

Once he got run over on his way across the road to another attack. When we rushed out to gather up his body there was a tyre mark along his side. This time the trip to the vet was very sombre indeed. He said that there was almost certainly internal damage and the best thing was to take him home, lie him in his bed and leave him to be quiet. He was clearly in shock, but tough, and he could be OK. Or he could die in a few hours. If he began to show obvious signs of pain we should bring him back to be put down.

At that point the police rang saying they had arrested someone for a burglary we had suffered a few days before and would we come now and identify them? Eric seemed to be comfortable so we rushed off.

The police had the wrong person. We got stuck in traffic. So when we got back home an hour or so later we expected to find him dead. In fact we could not find him at all. He was not in his bed. We checked to see if he had crawled to die under the sofa or behind the curtains. Nothing.

We had left the back door open (crazily now I think about it – this was London, we had just been burgled; but we were in a state of high disturbance) in case he needed to go out, and we went outside wondering if he had dragged himself into the garden. Indeed he had. Sort of.

We saw Eric, standing on the four-foot-high wall that ran along one side of the garden with a brick in his mouth. He wagged his tail when he saw us, dropped the brick at the back of the flower border and yapped urgently. It was the only time I was delighted to play that bloody game. He never showed any further sign of injury or pain. Terriers are very, very tough.

22. A Dog's View

Dogs do not compare how they feel now with past experience. As humans all our sensations, emotions and health are set against some standard that will vary greatly both individually and with time and circumstance. The way we feel today is only really measurable in terms of how we felt yesterday. Inevitably we transfer this to our dogs and assume they are feeling happier than they were or better than they will. They are not. They are just being, here and now. This enables them both to glory in the essence of the present and ignore the relative problems by which we are still measuring happiness and health.

Although dogs learn all kinds of things from experience, guilt – the sense of having done something wrong that will result in retribution – is not one of them. I know this goes against all the apparent evidence of a dog cringing in guilt with a chewed shoe in its bed, but your dog is two steps ahead of you and has adopted a submissive posture to soften your wrath. Because it is reading your body language before you are even aware that you are sending any messages out. The dog is not sorry for having done the deed, and almost certainly not aware of what it is that you are cross about, but is nevertheless very sorry indeed that you are cross.

It follows from this that there is little point in punishing a dog for something that it has done in your absence. It will take the punishment and show a lot of contrition, but not really understand what it is being punished for. In order for the punishment to be effective and fair in controlling future misdemeanours, you have to catch them red-handed.

The upside of this lack of guilt is that I do believe any dog will respond directly to mood and tone as well as very subtle indications like a nod or wink or slight tilt of the head. This means that the relationship between a dog and human can be extraordinarily subtle and intimate on an emotional as well as a practical level. When we say that 'my dog understands me', in many ways it does. A dog's emotional intelligence is far higher than that of many humans – but that does not mean that their intellectual brain is developed in the same way. They can know what you are thinking before you have verbalised it to yourself. They will know you are sad and share the burden of it, but never know why or what is making you feel that way.

This is of a piece with the extraordinary facility that dogs have to read signals from movement, tone, scent – especially scent – and mood. Dogs that are trained to respond to incipient epileptic fits are simply (or perhaps very complexly) reacting more sensitively than their owners.

Much more mundane, and probably more familiar to every dog owner, is the way that dogs seem to completely ignore one set of signals while reacting enthusiastically to others that, to the human perception at least, are remarkably similar. Nigel's monitoring of my unhurried breakfast always appears casual and indifferent. For instance if I get up and move to the stove he does not lift his head. But if I make exactly the same movement – or so it seems to me – and go to the sink, right next to the stove, he immediately rouses himself, stretches and wags his tail. The stove means breakfast is being made but the sink means it is being washed up and therefore over. Likewise if I go to the fridge, take out a jar and unscrew it he does not bat an eyelid. But lift the same jar from the table and screw the lid back on and he leaps up. Same action, give or take a clockwise thread, but he is able to read a completely different set of messages from it.

I also believe that dogs can truly, in any sense of the word, love their owners. This means that the relationship between a dog and a human can be deeply rich and rewarding for both parties. They are not 'just' an animal. They are the dearest of friends and part of our family. So when a criticism is levelled that someone treats their dogs 'like children', implying that this is a step too far, it may well be that this is appropriate and reasonable. Every pet dog has a role that can only be determined by each individual family.

The notion that an owner has to assume the role of leader of the pack, to be the alpha dog, with their pets submissive and therefore obedient, is a nonsense that is a complete misunderstanding of canine mentality. Dogs are not domesticated wolves but have evolved over tens of thousands of years to be a species in complete synchronicity with humans and dependent upon them. Bullying your dog into subdued obedience will result in a cowering, submissive animal. It is a relationship based upon fear pandering to the macho ego of the human.

As I've said before, this is not to say that dogs cannot, nor should not, be trained and obedient. There are parameters that make a family unit work and they have to be established and observed. Putting muddy feet on a clean sofa, stealing food, pooing in the corner, growling unpleasantly or shredding a favourite pair of shoes is pretty unacceptable behaviour from any family member, animal or human. But if you are happy with a clean dog sleeping down at the bottom of your bed, so be it. We have always had small dogs that rush upstairs in the morning, jump on the bed and burrow happily down to the bottom of the bedclothes, where they remain in a happy hot fug until we get up. Yet the same dogs know that they are not allowed upstairs at all during the rest of the day.

My son, the farmer, has a sheepdog called Meg. Meg is a nervous, highly strung dog, albeit with the sweetest of characters. She responds to the slightest look or intonation and is spooked by sudden noises or aggressive behaviour. Yet when she is working with the sheep – which she does with stunning skill – you have to be pretty firm and really shout at her at times to hold her back when required. A nod or calm voice would not do it. Yelling is appropriate in those circumstances, but would be destructive once she was away from the sheep.

I have hardly ever had to yell at Nigel. Training for TV work has been built entirely on his innate desire to please – with almost all carrot and very little stick.

23. The Greenhouse Yard

The greenhouse yard is effectively in the corner of the garden but is nevertheless its hub. Potting shed, greenhouse, workshop and cold frames all spin off its axis as well as the path round the end of the buildings to the front gardens, down the Long Walk and all the way up to the compost heaps at the far end.

As far as Nigel is concerned, the greenhouse is dull – just boring old plants; in fact mostly lovely, very young plants all above Nigel's eye level on staging. It smells of warmth, of slightly damp potting compost, and hundreds of plants breathing. The end section is a lark – the mist propagator will frequently erupt into mist. Nigel closes his eyes and lets the cloud coat his fur in a thousand droplets.

The potting shed is the place from which all energy and growth originate, and where I repair to when it gets too wet to garden outside. Every filming day has a potting shed item held in reserve as a kind of plan B if the weather gets too awful, although it is put into action surprisingly rarely. The tool shed is reached through the potting shed so, all in all, every action and every plant begins from this yard. And, for the record, the acoustics in the potting shed are ideal, so it is where I record all the voiceovers for *Gardeners' World*.

However great its virtues for the gardener and film crews, it has limited opportunities for good ball action, although jumping up so your paws hang over the edge of the potting tray and slowly rolling a saliva-slathered tennis ball from one's mouth into the potting mix does give it rather a nice coat of compost.

However, harsh words have been exchanged when Nigel's ball-dropping game involves dropping a compost-coated, soggy, heavy tennis ball on to a tray of fragile seedlings just as they have been put into a cold frame as part of their protected journey from a heated greenhouse to the exposed rigours of a border. A cold frame with its low brick wall is not only exactly the right height to stand over and plop a ball satisfyingly on to a pot, but is also clearly dull so needs livening up. Luckily for poor saps like me or anyone else working in the garden, Nigel is usually, and exceedingly annoyingly, on hand to do the livening.

For the record, I am a huge fan of cold frames and they are a key part of the way we raise many thousands of plants each year. They are cheap, adaptable and provide enough protection to over-winter tender plants and enough ventilation to harden off young plants in spring before planting them out. Ours are built of brick against a brick wall that we also built (there was another identical one on the other side of the box balls but it cast too much shade, so we pulled it down and used the bricks for the paths – which is why they are now all crumbling; every inch of the garden has layers of being), with lids made from double walled poly-something. The risk of slipping while holding a tray of plants makes big sheets of glass too dangerous.

Between the potting shed and the greenhouse is a table made from sixteen-feet-long scaffolding boards that we cover with bulbs in pots in spring – irises, muscari, fritillaries, hyacinths, daffodils, scillas and crocus. It also gets used as an extra-large work surface for sorting plants and potting up on nice days.

24. Mouth

Nigel's world is mediated by his mouth. It is as though things can only be made real by holding them – and the only way he can do that is to use his mouth.

If he really loves you then he has to get hold of you – preferably your hand – and cling to it for far longer than feels comfortable or natural. His teeth, biting rather too hard, have to be prised open so normal service can be resumed. He will often fall fast asleep with a ball or scrap of paper in his mouth, as though the default position is to clutch something – anything.

If he is at all scared or anxious the hand-biting is repeated, and this time there has to be a lot of stroking and back-rubbing, along with suitably comforting noises before he will let go voluntarily.

There is another kind of greeting which involves a frantic hunt for the one suitable object to pick up and bring to you. Until it is found there can be hardly any display of recognition, let alone greeting. What this offering might be is often baffling. Nigel will visit waste-paper baskets, his bed, underneath hedges and shrubs, growing increasingly busy and seemingly distracted from your presence, until he finds what he considers the ideal gift – which usually ends up being a scrunched-up envelope from a waste-paper basket or the current favoured yellow tennis ball. Then, and only then, can he properly come and say hello – groaning, wriggling and trying to bite your hand all at the same time, and all with the ball or piece of paper lodged firmly in his mouth.

His gift-giving has always had a highly refined core. From a small puppy he loved picking up tiny pieces of wood, like a matchstick, or a small object like a button or paperclip and bringing them to you, delicately lowering his head on to your seated lap while keeping his eyes fixed on yours. If you go to take the proffered object he darts his head away, playing very hard to get. Only when you have made sufficient failed attempts to snatch the titbit and then feigned a total lack of interest (not hard to do) is the absurdly small offering carefully spat on to your knee. Nigel then looks at you expectantly. The play has been made. It is now your turn.

If you ignore him it will be picked up and replaced with an impatient foot shuffle and a small, slightly incredulous bark. Come on! You know the rules. The game is to look at it, admire it profusely and then give it back. When you do – and you always do because he never, ever gives up – he takes it away, prancing, and returns to repeat the whole operation a few minutes later. And so it goes and will keep going – and going – until you surrender.

He has always been good at balancing things on his nose – and then catching them with his mouth. He does this by staying absolutely still after you have placed the object – usually something for him to eat – with his eyes fixed on you, waiting for the command that gives him permission to move.

The stillness is there whether he has to do the balancing trick or not – I notice Nell does exactly the same when waiting for her dinner, eyes locked on mine, lids immobile, frozen in anticipation, ready to move the millisecond she can go – and is all part of his eagerness to please, to do the right thing, and which has made him so easy to train. But the speed with which he can catch any object that he flicks from his muzzle is the real trick and all part of his incredible reflexes and dynamism. When Nigel wants something in his mouth he can move very fast indeed to get it there.

25. Noises

Nigel is noisy. He can do a proper grown-up bark when called upon that is surprisingly fierce – he has an iron fist inside his velvet glove and when roused will fight with an unexpected aggression – but by and large his noises are friendly, varied and very, very frequent. He talks a lot.

When he is sleepy he has a deep growly groan that rises to an unmanly bleat when excited, and when he is pleased to see you there will be a long sobbing welcome, often muffled by your hand as he holds it firmly in his mouth. Trying not to hurt his all too evident feelings, at the same time you find yourself fervently wishing he would stop. It is the equivalent of the man-hugs that start and have to be completed with slightly over-enthusiastic vigour, despite both parties being struck by embarrassment halfway through.

This greeting can be conferred on anyone Nigel has recently fallen in love with, which is as likely to be a complete stranger or a fresh member of the BBC crew as a member of the family he has known all his life.

The more surprised he is, the more vocal he becomes, with a welcoming bark in these situations that amounts to a shout. Nigel often goes off to spend the day farming with my son, and if I then go over and he discovers me in the farmyard, he greets me as if I have returned from walking across the Arctic.

What? *You!* Here? Why hello! What an unbelievable co-incidence! To stumble across each other in this place, on this day, at this time. *Amazing!*

And so the astounded barks become yelps and moans and the situation is not settled until a suitable amount of hand-biting has taken place.

Nigel has a particular going-for-a-walk sound, never taken from the Nigel sound archives in any other situation, that amounts to a whistle. It is a high-pitched exhalation that would be a squeak if it did not continue for so long. It is unmanly and I sense that he would rather not be making it. But it cannot be controlled. We are about to go for a walk. That calls for extreme noises.

It has never crossed Nigel's mind (and, even at his most perceptive, that is a short, uncomplicated journey) that he is not always the centre of attention. This means that when you are talking to someone or reading the paper, a slow rhythmic growling will start to build up as he tries to attract your attention. The sound is moderated by the size of ball in his mouth – a small one just adds a slight edge, whereas a large tennis ball means he has to blow harder to make the sound so it is a curious bass wheeze. This is repeated again and again, the same sound rising to a crescendo, at which point the growl is unmanned by a treble note of indignation that can become an all-out squealed bark. Then, when you catch his eye or ask him to be quiet, the ball is deposited on your lap and is, so to speak, now in your court. He has won.

In his mature years he regards luxury as a right, especially in the evening. Sometimes his bed will suffice but increasingly often he wants better. So if you are sitting on the sofa, reading or watching television, he will sit in front of you harrumphing with an exasperated drawn-out combination of sigh, growl and moan. If you ignore him, the sigh bit of the sound becomes protracted and increasingly sorrowful until the right note of tragedy is struck. Finally, bored by the canine opera, you then relent, and Nigel leaps up on to the sofa next to you, and unceremoniously and completely unapologetically edges you aside until he is really, properly comfy. At that point

there will be a long sigh and a basso growl of pleasure, and
Nigel Bear will sink into sleep in his rightful and proper bed.

26. The Jewel Garden

At the heart of Longmeadow is the Jewel Garden. It is not just the physical centre but an ideological and psychological one too. It is a big, difficult space to keep looking good and so we have invested an awful lot of thought, time and effort into it. It is very high maintenance and very demanding. While it can look spectacular, it can also easily become chaotic and rambling, like an overworked painting. It is not so much a well-oiled machine as a distinctly temperamental thoroughbred.

The original plan for that part of the garden was to be a circular lawn surrounded by a yew hedge. I duly planted the yews and mowed the grass, but it was never very convincing. Some things never fit, however much you want them to or however good an idea they seem on paper. Making a garden is as much about finding it and letting it reveal itself to you as constructing or taming it.

Because I had cleared it from a tussocky mix of grass and brambles, I had made the assumption that the lawn was an 'improvement' – a kind of horticultural award that I was bestowing on it. But beneath the lawn was superb soil. Grass was not going to be good enough for it. So out came the yew, off came the grass, and Sarah and I started planning a range of borders with a distinct theme.

Throughout the 1980s Sarah and I set up and ran a costume jewellery business, designing everything we made for fashion shows, films, theatre, bands, an opera and our own shop, as well as hundreds of stores we sold to around the world. Then, to cut a long and muddly story short, it collapsed around us, leaving us blinking in the wreckage, having sold our business, house, furniture and everything we owned that had any financial value, to cover the debts. Eventually we ended up at a ruined farmhouse with a couple of acres of untended pasture attached to it. This was Longmeadow in 1991.

That story is well documented in our book *The Jewel Garden* and, with a quarter of a century's hindsight, feels like Life. Things happen. You get over it and move on. But at the time we were still raw with what had been a very painful experience. However, after a few years, and when we had settled into Longmeadow, we realised that if we could make a beautiful garden from an ugly experience, then something good and meaningful would have come from it. So we decided to make a Jewel Garden that would use the colours of jewellery, including gold, silver, copper and bronze. In practice this is more a case of editing out what we do not use in this part of the garden than what we do. So, no whites, pinks, lilacs, mauves, lemon yellows or pale blues. In theory. In practice, rogue colours creep in and stay in, cheerfully breaking the rules. But deciding on a palette is a good restriction to impose on a border. It gives a framework to edit from and editing is the key to almost all planting.

It was – as indeed is the whole garden – a shared project. We have always allowed each other a veto on any plan. In order to make it happen we have to convince the other to agree. This applies to every detail. It slows things down and makes for some quite spiky arguments, but it also means that you have to really think through and inspect what you want to do, and when it does happen there is real and lasting consensus. It is an important part of our marriage, and the pleasure of gardening with someone you love and respect is endlessly rewarding.

Now this is all highfalutin', dramatic stuff. But, looking at it another way, you could say that we were making a series of flower beds and decided to give them a bit of a theme. True. Every gardener does that in one way or another. But I think that it is important to bring as much personal meaning as possible to your garden. That meaning can be quirky or very private but, without it, gardens are bland. It is the difference between a hotel room and a home.

So the circle of grass became a square of eight long borders that then lost the paths dividing them and evolved into eight large square beds which were then extended to add another four big beds – which have since been separated off again to become the grass borders.

We wanted each bed to be like an open jewel box, spilling over with an extravagance of enticing colour. To achieve this effect we decided to edge each border with box and bought 500 plants at a pound apiece. I remember that it felt like betrayal because we had always bought plants in dribs and drabs and propagated everything we possibly could. I raised another thousand plants from cuttings and, after a couple of years, all the beds were edged. Within five years these had become crisp, solid hedges. In fact quite a few of those hedges were removed when we began to film *Gardeners' World* at Longmeadow in order to widen the paths so cameras and kit could get down them. But, as ever in a garden, forced change brings opportunity. We now have paths that can be edged with low plants rather than having to have everything tall enough to rise above the box.

This phase of the Jewel Garden grew and thrived for about eight years. It took a lot of work to maintain, with hundreds of annuals grown and added each season, mulching each spring with twenty tons of mushroom compost that took endless barrows to shift from the drive where it was dumped, and almost constant weeding and cutting back. But that is gardening. It is what we all love and it looked fantastic and gave us huge pleasure. Around the time we got Nigel, the summer of 2008, we let the Jewel Garden slip. We had no help in the garden; I had been extremely busy then unwell for a while, and it quickly became overgrown with bindweed and the lovely but thuggish ornamental bramble *Rubus thibet-anus*. So at the end of 2010 we dug the whole thing up and started again. It will need similar treatment again very soon.

The borders are completely mixed, with a range of plants from bananas to wallflowers via tender perennials such as cannas and dahlias, annuals by the thousand, robust herbaceous perennials, a forest of alliums and tulips in spring, small trees such as the weeping silver pear, *Pyrus salicifolia*, and purple hazels, shrubs such as buddleia, lilac and sambucus, and a lot of clematis all growing up bean sticks cut from the coppice.

We now have eight large pots that are planted as set pieces every May – cannas, dahlias and cosmos always look good, and we have used phormiums and fuchsias in the past, as well as topiarised holly and Portuguese laurel. In winter these pots are planted with tulips beneath wallflowers. But in winter the Jewel Garden is essentially put away and, if it is dry enough – which is only one year in three – we cut it back, move plants, and mulch it in November and let it sleep until the new growth appears at the end of March.

But it is not an institution. It does not seamlessly roll from season to season on a well-worn track. Plants outgrow their position, they die or, as has so dramatically happened to all the box hedging that is such an important part of the struc-ture, they get attacked by disease. The garden changes a little and, before you know, it drifts away from you. Having made a garden from scratch and tended it for twenty-five years, I realise that changes – big changes – are inevitable.

Nigel has seen the Jewel Garden change more than anything else in this garden. But every spadeful that I dug to make the borders over one winter (in between trips abroad for the *Holiday* programme, coming back tanned and spoilt from a flit to the Bahamas), going out into the dank December mud, was accom-panied by another beloved dog called Beaufort. From when we first came here in October 1991, until his death six years later, I never set foot outside without Beaufort coming along too, and he, along with two other of our dogs, remains in the garden, buried in the coppice just next to the Jewel Garden.

27. Damp Garden, Wet Dog

I remember having a picnic at Longmeadow in April 1992, when the children were tiny. The house was a building site and we were living in a rented farmhouse a mile or so up the road. I had just cut the grass of the two-acre field for the first time. Beaufort lolled to one side, eyeing the sandwiches. I planted a few primroses near where we ate our sandwiches, and the children helped me push some willow cuttings into the soft soil along the boundary where the ground was still wet from recent flooding.

Those willow cuttings, then the size of a pencil, are now forty-foot trees; when we cut one down to make the pond, we needed to hire a stump grinder to excavate the roots. Be careful what you wish for.

The primroses were dug up and shifted, first to the Spring Garden, and then to the coppice, where they have all regularly been divided and moved; but perhaps the same plants are still flowering there.

The site of that first picnic was what came to be called the Damp Garden.

We called it the Damp Garden because it is the first part of the garden to flood, and consequentially has always been planted with moisture-loving plants such as hostas, ligularias, rodgersias, shuttlecock ferns, candelabra primulas and camassias. Quinces are one of the few fruit trees that can thrive in moist soil, and there are four different varieties planted at the back of the pond, as well as a 'Tai-haku' cherry and a spreading *Viburnum plicatum* f. *tomentosum* 'Mariesii'. It is, above all, ideal for hostas, and they grow enormous and unmarked by slug or snail. My theory is that the combination of a really good winter soak – from the flooding – and rich soil means that they will tolerate a good deal of summer drought, although chance would be a fine thing . . .

The shuttlecock or ostrich fern, *Matteuccia struthiopteris*, has become a fairly intrusive weed in this part of the garden, popping up from its long black stoloniferous runners all over the place, but always attractively, and so far has never crept into another part of the garden – although this spring I did dig some up and transplant them to the shadiest part of the orchard beds. When mature it forms a little trunk, like a mini tree fern but entirely hardy. Its one weakness is in wind, which will snap and damage the foliage as though a dog has been rampaging through after a ball (which has also been known to happen . . .).

The pond was late to arrive. After the first year's filming at Longmeadow, we had a planning meeting (so short the life, so many the BBC meetings), and it was put to me that we ought to have a pond. I said that we did. Blank looks round the table. Well, I said, stick around and a bloody big pond will come along next time it floods. Very beautiful it is too.

I was not being entirely facetious. We have lived with flooding throughout our time here. It literally comes with the territory. There has never felt like a shortage of water at Longmeadow. Also the fields, when flooded, make such a dramatic and noble lake that anything we might create would seem puny in comparison. So we were quite happy to 'borrow' the occasional pond presented erratically but reliably literally on our doorstep.

There have been a couple of ponds previously in this garden. But they were not garden ponds as such. Both were purely functional, designed only to give our ducks (and, inevitably, Nigel) a place to swim and splash about. The fox – as he has done before – took all the ducks, and I could not bring myself to replace their charming selves and go through the business of finding their decapitated bodies scattered around the orchard, so the pond remained unused, empty of everything save water. Fallen apples bobbed in the scummy water and it remained abandoned and unloved, a testimony to the painful absence of ducks rather than any horticultural presence.

I did have a tiny pond inside the plastic tunnel that stood where the top veg patch is. It was planted only with a fringe of nettles, and again its role was purely functional, existing to add humidity to the air and to attract frogs and toads to eat slugs. It worked very well and I highly recommend a pond, however small – this was about the size of a dustbin lid – inside all but the smallest polytunnel.

In the end, though, we made a pond which now dominates the Damp Garden. It is lovely and attracts a mass of dragon-flies, frogs, newts, birds and bats – all of which enrich the garden and the gardener. The repertoire of the garden is expanded for television, and all the plants that we grew there before are just as happy and look even better set against the water.

However, there was one small problem with siting it, and

that was the path that had run through the middle of that area, crossed the Long Walk, continued through the grass borders and on to the Mound. I liked it. I liked the way that this narrow strip cut through and drew your eye on. I did not want to lose it. Yet, short of a walkway over the water, possible but tricky, I could not have path and pond. However, I realised that if I made the pond very shallow directly under the line of the path and kept it free of any growth, the light would reflect off the water and continue the line. Which it does – and I have the memory of the path lit in evening sun.

Nigel has so far resisted the temptation to plunge in, although he occasionally stands at the edge looking at the frogs and water beetles with mild interest; perhaps only the availability of the river and frequent flooding has stopped him cooling off in it.

We still flood, pond and all. When the ground is saturated – which here can be for months on end in a wet winter – Longmeadow becomes a sodden place. There have been many years when in midwinter we have hardly been able to walk in the garden for weeks at a time, let alone cultivate it. But with this wetness comes a beauty that transforms the landscape and always seems like a privileged bonus. The higher the flood, the more beautiful it is. There has been a house on the site for at least a thousand years, and the people who chose the site knew what they were about. We are right on the edge of the flood plain – but not on it. The water comes up past the kitchen window and has reached six inches from the back door, but never yet come inside, and when we dug down well below the floor level twenty-five years ago, there was no evidence at all of any historical flooding.

So we live with the wetness and count our blessings. And no one appreciates it more than Nigel. Whether in deep flood, or the vast puddles the size of large garden ponds that remain for months in the fields, Nigel will splosh all day long, seemingly impervious to wet or cold.

28. Accident

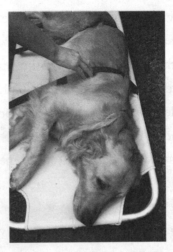

I t was a gentle morning in September and I was slowly
addressing myself to an article that I hoped to finish
in good time before a long and sunny weekend. But the
scream was a shattering alarm call and sent me running
downstairs from my work room and rushing outside,
thinking there had been an accident to one of the two
gardeners and that they would need immediate and
perhaps emergency attention. I remember hearing voices
but not being able to find anyone at all within the hedged
maze of the garden.

Eventually I found one of them, Julia, at the edge of the

Jewel Garden, crouched over the body of Nigel, who was shaking violently and crying.

What had happened was completely, freakishly unexpected. For the thousandth time Nigel carefully placed a muddy yellow ball on the clipped level top of the box hedge next to Julia as she cut back spent dahlia flowers in the Jewel Garden. She, as she had done a thousand times before, without looking up, flicked it away sideways for him to chase and Nigel leapt in the air to take it, twisting sideways and up with astonishing speed and dynamism. As he had done so many times before. But then he suddenly screamed – loudly enough for me to hear inside the house a hundred yards away – and fell, and by the time he hit the ground he was paralysed.

I immediately rang the vet and told them what had happened.

'If you would like to bring him in after surgery, the small animals' vet will see him then.'

How long would that be?

'About another two hours.'

'But this is an emergency. Can a vet come out?'

'Not till later this morning, I am afraid, when he has completed his surgery.'

She was friendly and polite but immovable. I rang off, exasperated.

I stroked Nigel's head, not knowing what to do other than

164

not to move him and to stop him trying to move himself. All around us the garden was in its late summer pomp, the day becoming glorious, but at that moment I would have traded it for a cramped concrete yard to have Nigel stretch and clamber back to his feet with a rueful and slightly embarrassed expression. This was entirely fanciful. He lay, quivering, crying and clearly in a state of shock.

After five endless minutes I rang the vet again.

'This is an acute emergency,' I said. 'I really need a vet now.'

I heard a discussion going on over the hushed noise of the veterinary waiting room.

The receptionist came back to the phone. 'OK,' she said. 'If it is a matter of life and death we will send emergency nurses. Hold on. They will be with you in about ten minutes.'

So we held on, awaiting the crack team. I half expected a helicopter or the canine equivalent of mountain rescue. In fact, after barely ten minutes, two charming ladies, as unassuming and quietly competent as a 1960s WI outing, arrived with a collapsible stretcher. By this time Nigel was shaking violently, clearly in a state of shock. I had covered him with a couple of lurid dog-drying towels that added a touch of garish absurdity to the situation. With great efficiency they got Nigel on to the stretcher and took him into the surgery, where he was given a huge injection of steroids to reduce any swelling and then kept under observation. We were told that there was nothing we could do but wait until the morning when they would assess the damage.

The next morning I rang to see how he was.

'He's fine. But one leg has had it.'

I went to collect him and, although pleased to see me, one leg dragged uselessly behind him, bent in on itself, the knuckle scraping appallingly on the gravel. The vet said he might well have to amputate it as there was little chance of recovery and 'It will only get in the way.' But he wanted to see what other potential damage had been done as, if his abdomen and bowel had been affected, there was nothing they could do. In any event, he added, without a scan it would be hard to tell and a scan was very expensive and involved travelling to Liverpool.

Nigel slept most of the day and then, as a reaction to the steroids and shock, proceeded to have a violently upset tummy all night long. A dog with uncontrollable, bloody diarrhoea is bad, but one unable to move sufficiently to avoid soiling himself, the floor, the walls and the people trying to help him is very bad indeed. On top of that he was clearly going down-hill. Nigel was partially paralysed, completely dehydrated and was reducing in front of our eyes to skin and bone. He seemed dangerously close to death.

The next day we got him to drink a little and the diarrhoea subsided. But he was pitifully weak, incontinent and one leg dangled from him like a piece of string. We had all been up all night and were exhausted, shocked and upset.

Outside the sun blazed. Longmeadow – Nigel's garden – had never looked lovelier.

~

That night I rang a friend who said that she knew a vet who specialised in extreme cases. By then it was late on Sunday evening, but she said he was an extraordinary man and would respond if he could. Almost by return I received an email from the vet himself, Noel Fitzpatrick. He would see Nigel at ten the next morning but he needed a referral from my local vet. When I rang for this he asked who the referral was to. I said Noel Fitzpatrick. 'Wow !' said our local vet. 'You've got friends in high places. He's the very best.' It was exactly what I wanted to hear.

So early the next morning, after a relatively calm night, Sarah and my youngest son drove Nigel the hundred and fifty miles from Longmeadow to Godalming in the Surrey countryside, where Noel Fitzpatrick's centre, Fitzpatrick's Referrals, is based. I waited, having to work to meet deadlines, trying not to raise my expectations and telling myself that lots of dogs live happy lives with three legs. But for all my pragmatism, the outlook was pretty grim.

However, they returned later that afternoon buoyant and full of optimism. It was, they said, an extraordinary place, fitted with the latest and most modern technology coupled with the most straightforwardly caring staff and a prevailingly positive attitude. They were convinced that if anyone could do anything, then he could. They had waited while a CAT scan was done and Noel viewed the result. He was immediately able to tell them what had happened. When Nigel leapt in the air, the speed and acceleration were so powerful and he twisted with such suppleness that one of the discs in his back exploded apart and the fluid within it was shot out with the velocity of a bullet and cut through his spinal cord, partially severing it.

The scan had shown his spinal cord with a wedge cut out from it like a slice of cake.

Although unusual, this was not unknown. Apparently it did occasionally happen, as dramatically and suddenly as it had done to Nigel, to particular types of young, large but very fit and lean dogs with exceptional dynamic power – i.e. the ability to leap with explosive elasticity. Nigel fitted the bill exactly. The power generated by such leaping, when combined with a sudden twist, was enough to burst the disc and effectively break the dog's own back.

Noel would not operate but kept him in the correct position, coupled with hydrotherapy several times a day in the pool. This involved two nurses taking him into the heated water and getting him to gently swim to maintain movement without any weight bearing.

Noel rang me that night. In his strong Irish brogue, he went straight to the point. 'His leg is completely dead from the hip down. We will keep him in for five days and, though I can't promise anything, I think he'll be fine.'

Five days later we went to collect him and Nigel walked out to the car, tail up, wanting to leap into the back. Five days earlier we had been told, by a good and trusted vet, that his leg should probably be amputated. It seemed little short of miraculous.

Noel gave us strict instructions for his aftercare. For six weeks he must stay on a lead. Four walks a day of twenty minutes each. Strictly no running or jumping whatsoever. Then increase that to two walks a day of an hour – still on a lead – for a couple of weeks, and then at the end of those eight weeks Nigel would be as good as he was going to get.

Because of the wedge shape of the damage, there was a real chance of that thin end of the wedge re-growing and fusing. At the fatter end there would remain permanent damage, the extent of which only time would tell; but sticking to the prescribed routine would maximise recovery.

The chances of it happening again, Noel said, were quite high – about 20 per cent. But the chances of him living a long, active life were much higher. And once Nigel had made a full recovery, we should discourage any jumping, but not mollycoddle him. If his spine went again as a result of a sudden and dramatic leap, then so be it. He was still a young, fit dog and it would be a good way to go.

And so began six weeks of Nigel walking everywhere – even indoors for the first few weeks, on a lead so that he would not run or leap. He had hardly ever been on a lead before. Because we live in the middle of fairly remote countryside, we only took a lead with us on walks as a precaution if we did come across other dogs, but that rarely ever happened. Going for a walk meant that we walked but Nigel ran – and ran and ran. If there was time we would both walk for miles, with Nigel quadrupling the amount of ground I covered. If time was short we played cricket.

Nigel liked football, was very happy to play rugby, and of course was addicted to tennis – but he really, *really* loved cricket. It involved me setting off across the fields with my old school cricket bat and a few tennis balls in my pocket and whacking them as far as I could. I would pretend to be disdainfully dispatching the very best that the Aussies could offer, into the stands over long-on or midwicket at Lords, and Nigel would run as fast as he could, bring it back so it could all happen again, and again, until I would worry about his heart and we would ease back a bit. He became very fit indeed.

Perhaps that was the problem. Had he been less highly tuned he might not have had the incredible dynamic energy needed to go from a standing start to bursting open his own spine in a single leap.

So this enforced restriction was hard. It quickly became a tyranny, with Nigel bored to tears and completely unable to work out why he was suddenly tethered to the lead.

But I stuck with it to the letter and treated it as a regime that I was as bound to as Nigel. The only variation came on filming days, which were Wednesdays and Thursdays, when I would take him at first light, again when we broke for lunch, and immediately we wrapped at six. Because the days were becoming rapidly shorter, the opportunities to walk were increasingly reduced, and the fourth outing on those days was lost to darkness.

Other than a tremor in his afflicted leg, which he has retained, and an inability to cock that leg, it did not seem to trouble him at all. In fact the biggest problem – for him – revealed itself slowly, which was that he could not scratch himself with that leg, so now he rubs his head and chin forcibly on the ground, ideally on hard or frosty grass. His very sensitive skin means that he can easily wear it down to the flesh.

By the end of November the rehabilitation was complete. Nigel was moving freely off the lead and running without a trace of a limp. The fields flooded in the November rains and he swam and splashed across them exactly as he had done before. He was healed.

Of course Nigel had no concept of being healed or being injured. Bits worked as they did when they did. A leg out of action was clearly a nuisance, but he adapted accordingly without any reference to his former self. But I did. I wanted the old Nigel Bear back and was very, very happy to have this slightly revamped version, marked a little by the vicissitudes of life, but not changed.

29. The Supervet

A couple of months later I drove Nigel down to Godalming to see Noel Fitzpatrick for a check-up. He cast an eye over him, watched him walk across the car park, felt his spine, prodded a little and pronounced himself pleased. Nigel was fully discharged.

With Nigel lying at my feet I chatted to Noel while he worked. This is the only way he can talk because, as far as I can gather, he only stops work to sleep – and does very little of that. I talked to him for nearly two hours in his office. His desk is set up with seven large computer screens and piles of papers, artificial joints and bones. The floor is barely passable for more papers, sports kit and cardboard boxes. He toys with a plate of food throughout, which was, at four p.m., his lunch. While I'm with him, his phone rings every two minutes and he answers with curt, precise instructions, most technically detailed as though his caller is in mid-operation (there are six senior surgeons and six interns working in the theatres). A secretary knocks and enters every five minutes with papers to sign. Interns in surgical gowns come and ask questions. He rings a cat owner and gently tells her the extent of her pet's injuries. The X-ray is up on one of the screens. It looks as though there is internal scaffolding holding the animal together. I can hear the woman weeping and Noel gently but calmly comforting her.

It reminds me of nothing so much as a flight controller guiding in an endless stream of planes – while also having to repair the engines and fly them himself. He lives, eats, sleeps and breathes his work.

At one point I listened while he arranged to meet an intern to go through an academic paper. 'I am free from midnight till three on Sunday,' he said. 'Yes, I know it is late. But it is the only time. And it must be done.'

As well as working a hundred hours a week in this practice, he travels widely and conducts research programmes in America.

When they made a television series about Noel they called

him, in the hyperbolic way that television cannot resist, *The Supervet*, but in truth he is no ordinary vet.

I shared a house at university with a vet student, so I met many other trainee vets in that time and, having owned domestic and farm animals most of my life, I have had to use the services of many different vets in my time. Almost all are admirable, but none are like Noel Fitzpatrick.

The clinic is certainly extraordinary, with its hydrotherapy pool where dogs swim their way to recovery, its Perspex-sided kennels with televisions for company and regular visits from nurses talking to each animal, its lecture theatre and over a hundred staff in total. There are also the amazing 'bionic' operations fixing titanium prosthetics into existing bone to provide false limbs, so smashed bodies are reassembled and bolted back together.

Although that kind of extreme surgery is unusual, it is not unknown – not least because animals can be experimented upon and repaired without most of the moral burden loaded on to humans undergoing disaster surgery. But there is a reluctance to cross-reference between animal and human surgery – although doctors are finding the work that has been done repairing animals can have direct and practical application.

'I can experiment on animals,' Noel says. 'If, after exploring every moral and ethical aspect, the only choice is your pet dying or me giving it a chance of a longer, happy life by trying something new, then you might make that choice. It is not mine to make, but I have to offer it. If it is successful then much of what we learn in the process can be applied to humans. It is a case of saving an animal life to save a human life. But we are not making those cross-references.'

I say that this surgery is hugely expensive. Is he very rich? Noel laughs. 'No one trains to be a vet to get rich,' he says. 'I have not taken a wage for ten years.' He is certainly the most driven, unmaterialistic man I have ever met. 'Ninety-five per cent of all our work is routine and exactly the same as any other practice. We just do it very well. The five per cent of prosthetic and experimental work costs a lot to do and does not make any money. The costs are the same as human surgery and care – and often significantly better. Everybody is looked after all the time. But it is important.'

The truly amazing thing about Noel Fitzpatrick is that he is a man who loves animals and believes that this love – together with the love that we receive in return from our pets – is the most important thing in the world. This is not how most vets think, and the few that do hardly say as much. By and large sick animals are viewed objectively with all human emotion stripped away. There is a sound logic behind this because the weight and strain of emotional involvement, added to the intensity with which someone like Noel

Fitzpatrick works, is beyond endurance for most normal people.

But Noel is anything but normal. He is a brilliant technician, extremely hard-working, with a cold, clear brain, as single-minded as any human being I have met, and yet is also a deeply emotional man who – and this is the thing that makes him really unusual – is not in the least ashamed or covert about these emotions. He walks a fine tightrope between intense passion and a clear-eyed practical application of knowledge and skill. But one of his catchphrases is, 'They don't care what you know until they know that you care.' And boy, does he care. He says that anthropomorphism is a dirty word, especially with vets, but it should not be. He believes with every fibre of his being that the love we share with our pets is real and a powerful force for human good. So he treats the animals in his care with the same detail and focus as any human in a hospital would be treated.

One of his passions is to harness all the scientific discoveries and exploration in his fields – which he says vets scarcely acknowledge, let alone employ – with the compassion and empathy needed for true healing. He is explicit that, for him, working with animals is an unparalleled opportunity to expand our treatment of humans, because all animal health relates to human health.

Until Noel did it, no vet had considered making the kennels of clear Perspex so the animals could see what was going on. The kennels are warm, friendly and gently soothing – all the things that any sick creature needs before or after a major operation. The end result is not just that it is ethical but that the animal recovers far quicker. Noel also understands instinctively that every sick animal – and some of the animals he treats have the most appalling injuries – brings with it a distraught owner. The two cannot be separated. He says, 'You have to have empathy. If that is anthropomorphic, then so be it. There must be real feeling. You have to hold hands – yet veterinary training used to be unfeeling and coldly scientific.'

The intensity of the man is like a powerful electrical charge, but it is consuming him as fast as it is driving the world revolving around him. The pressure is constant, immense. How does he cope? When I ask him this he points to large letters on the wall behind his desk that spell out: 'All You Need Is Love'.

'That is the truth,' he says. 'Everything else is bullshit. If people would only realise this then we could change everything.'

What he is talking about is very simple. Every single pet owner shares this view. We love our pets and they love us. Life would be immeasurably poorer without them. By the same token they are representatives of every creature on this

Nigel has never really lost the innocent sweetness of when he was a little puppy.

Nigel's first solo foray into the garden, braving the step down into the Lime Walk.

Nigel drenched with dew on his first walk when he was just twelve weeks old.

Nigel at four months old. He grew fast and by late summer had the gangly muscularity and clumsiness of a teenager.

For the first four years of his life Nigel was astonishingly athletic, with an elastic dynamism that meant he could leap anything with ease.

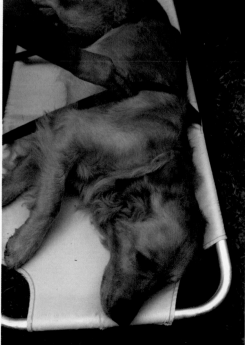

Nigel strapped to a stretcher after breaking his back whilst leaping for a ball in the Jewel Garden. By the time he landed he was paralysed and in agony. His subsequent recovery is little short of miraculous.

Golden retrievers were originally bred to fetch game from deep and difficult water, and as long as the 'game' is a ball or a stick Nigel will happily swim all day.

Nigel's one attempt at being a sheepdog consisted of a friendly but fruitless introduction to this ram, who remained unmoved.

Happy boy.

Nigel spent years of application in becoming a master of relaxation,
ranging from the deep luxury of a sofa to the watchful, patient
pose that he is ready to spring up from at the hint of a walk.

One of my favourite pictures of Nigel at the head of the Lime Walk. There is, of course, a ball at the top of the steps.

Nigel and I on the path between the Jewel Garden and the Grass Borders. Going in this direction has the possibility of continuing through the garden out into the fields. Hence the spring in his step.

Nigel has an uncanny knack of striking a fetching pose whenever a camera – especially a television camera – is around. I had no intention of including him in this picture but by the time I had climbed the wall for my vantage point he had strategically positioned himself.

I did not know he was in this picture of the Box Balls (pre box blight) until I reviewed it later and realised he was racing through in pursuit of a ball.

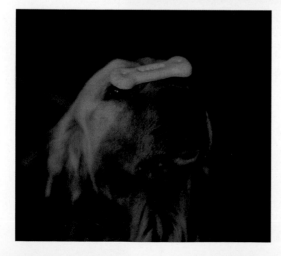

Nigel may not be the sharpest knife in the drawer and is hopelessly gunshy and often gets in a muddle, but he can balance things on his nose, flick them up and catch them. Every time. Which makes up for a lot.

In November 2015 Nellie joined the household at Longmeadow. Nell spent a lot of time asleep in my arms.

Early training. Even the smallest biscuit works wonders for a puppy's concentration. And Nigel's.

Nigel was never less than gentlemanly and tolerant but clearly thought it a bit rich that he had to share his bed with a disrespectful pup.

planet of which, eventually, humans are just one more. If that cycle of affection that so clearly heals and improves all life can best be served by Noel Fitzpatrick in a veterinary theatre, then that is where he is to be found.

'Look,' Noel says, 'the only things that matter are love and health. That's it! There is nothing else.'

30. The Vegetable Garden

There was a time, in the pre-Nigel era, when we grew a lot more vegetables at Longmeadow than we do now. There were growing mouths to feed and we seemed to have a little more time to store surplus produce, making sauces, chutneys, soups and juices and freezing them in large quantities. The Cottage Garden was entirely vegetables for the first twenty years, and where the wooden greenhouse now stands were raised beds and a large polytunnel where the raised beds are. We had lots more soft fruit, and where the nursery beds are now was overspill for crops like potatoes and squashes that take up a lot of room.

The polytunnel went long ago, but we have one greenhouse devoted to tomatoes and basil in summer and salad crops in winter, and the wooden one has a vine as well as being a good place to grow chillies, aubergines, and melons in pots. But our vegetables have been refined over the years. I grow less for storage and more for eating fresh when ready. Asparagus is wonderful in May and June, broad beans in June and July and squashes, celery and sweetcorn belong to September and October. Everything in its season, and when that season is finished then we are happy to wait until it comes around again. By careful choice of varieties, and managing the growing conditions, favourites such as lettuce can be grown pretty much year round and the winter kales, cabbages, beets and roots are welcome in an earthy way that is less appealing in summer when one craves green freshness above all else.

And there is expansion. New vegetable beds have been laid out and are filling with the more unusual and harder-to-find varieties – many of them heirloom and in danger of being lost in the absurdly monolithic bureaucracy that controls what seeds can and cannot be sold. These new beds hark back to the ones that I made when we first came here, edged with woven hazel, inspired by the medieval and Tudor beds that are clear in paintings of the period and certainly would have been used when the house was built.

I have always grown lots of soft fruit and regard raspberries, gooseberries, redcurrants, blackcurrants and rhubarb as life-enhancing treats in whatever form they can be eaten.

Nigel is very partial to a strawberry or two and will quietly help himself if there is no anti-blackbird netting to stop him. But there is one treat in the vegetable garden that he finds irresistible and will go to some lengths to sneak away and avail himself of, and those are peas. Nigel adores peas, preferably eaten while still attached to the vine.

31. Pea Thief

Nigel was born in May and arrived at Longmeadow in early July. This meant that by the time he was old enough to get out and about unsupervised, the pea season was over. However, he has done his best to make up for that initial deprivation ever since.

Between mid-June and late July he can often be found standing, all but hidden, between two rows of peas growing up pea sticks like twiggy leguminous hedges, carefully biting off pea pods and crunching them up with evident relish. He is quite picky about those he eats. Too young and they do not have enough body; too old, the pods are flabby and the peas inside floury and hard, and they are rejected out of hand. So he selects carefully, a discriminating gourmet knowing exactly what he is looking for, and then relishing every mouthful.

He is in exalted company in his veneration of the pea. Louis XIV, the Sun King, had a huge vegetable garden, the Potager du Roi, made between 1678 and 1683 at Versailles. It covered almost twenty-five acres, with twenty-nine different walled enclosures, and almost every kind of fresh fruit and vegetable grown – the more out of season and earlier it was produced on the king's table the better. But nothing pleased Louis more than a dish of fresh peas. Fresh peas were a luxury and became a fetish of his. His mistress, Madame de Sévigné, wrote in a letter that 'the pea business still goes on. Impatience to eat them, the pleasure of having eaten them and the hope to eat more of them are the three questions constantly discussed . . .'

Thomas Jefferson, third president of the United States, author of the American Declaration of Independence, a Founding Father, and one of the towering figures of Western civilisation, grew as many as fifteen different varieties of peas in his garden at Monticello, and he would compete with his Virginian neighbours to see who could produce the first dish of peas, the winner hosting a meal where this dish would be consumed and admired by all.

One of my own heroes, William Cobbett, who was a contemporary of Jefferson's, was also much taken with the business of growing peas. Cobbett wrote one book about gardening – *The English Gardener* – published in 1833, seven years after Jefferson's death, and in it he shares the American's fanaticism for peas, as early in the season as possible, saying, 'Ever since I became a man, I can recollect that it was always deemed rather a sign of bad gardening if there were not green peas in the garden fit to gather on the fourth of June.'

Well, we have never had peas ready to harvest by the fourth of June, although they are usually ready by the end of that month and can be picked into August.

Not all dogs like peas. I remember that my Labrador Gretel, as greedy and unfussy as any dog might ever be, would carefully lick around any peas in her food bowl, and if you gave her one would munch it carefully and slowly, as if looking for any traces of pleasure before spitting it out pristine and apparently untouched.

But I suspect Nigel watches the peas growing as carefully as I do, checking out the shift from flower to pod and watching them swell and fill with peas until that perfect moment when they become a succulent green doggy snack.

32. Baffin and Beaufort

It was the middle of a cold night in January 1988 and I was heading down the long road home from Scotland, feeling empty, sad and confused. I was certain I had done the right thing. It was best for everybody. Yet I regretted it terribly.

I had found my lovely dog, Baffin, the best possible home that any large, confident dog could have. I had reared and cared for Baffin from an eight-week pup to a fully grown, two-year-old magnificent animal, over three feet high at the shoulder, weighing around 100 pounds and full of joyful life. Now Baffin had the sea to swim in, hundreds of acres of moorland to roam, and kind, good people to care for his every need.

But I missed him already. He had never spent more than half an hour apart from his brother, Beaufort, before we had driven up to Scotland the day before. Were they missing each other? And as these thoughts ran through my mind on the 400-mile drive to London in the January wind and rain, I knew they were a self-pitying, anthropomorphic indulgence. He was a dog. He lived entirely in the present, and the present that I had placed him into was a kind of dog-heaven. I had two other dogs, both of whom would be happier in the less-competitive set-up. Most important of all, my children would be safer. Sarah would be less anxious. Everything and everybody benefited.

But I still felt a profound and heartbroken sense of loss.

Two years earlier I remember taking a pad of paper and drawing a line down the middle. On one side I wrote Pros and the other Cons. The latter came first and was long:

- Too big
- Very expensive
- Got quite enough on our plate already
- Very smelly
- Got two dogs already

- First baby due soon
- House and garden too small
- Ridiculously romantic
- Actually just ridiculous.

In the Pros column there were just two entries:

- Beautiful
- Will live off raw fish

It was no contest. The raw fish swung it, and in January 1986 we went to collect two large bundles of black fluff, each the size of a fully grown spaniel. They were Baffin and Beaufort, the two blackdog brothers.

It had all begun at the end of December 1979, when I was shopping in the little fishing town of Whitby on the North Yorkshire coast, a few miles from where Sarah and I were then living. I saw a good friend of mine, Jonathan Conville, disappear round the corner just ahead of me. This was unexpected because I knew he was in Switzerland, climbing the Matterhorn. So I ran after him, thinking that perhaps the trip had been abandoned and he had come instead to Yorkshire to visit. When I turned the corner the street was empty. It was very strange.

The next day I heard that Jonathan had fallen to his death from the mountain two days before.

Next to my chair in my study is his Eko twelve-string guitar. It is not a very good instrument and I play it as badly as he did, but his mother gave it to me and I would not sell it for any imaginable sum of money, or exchange it for any other object. Apart from anything else, it means I think of him every day and remember when I had to listen to his terrible guitar playing and even worse singing.

Jonathan's girlfriend, Marie Claire Foa, became a good friend of Sarah's and mine after his death. Marie Claire is an artist and she went off in the summer of 1982 to join the Transglobe expedition in the Arctic as expedition artist. So through her we got to know Ran and Ginny Fiennes, whose brainchild the vertical navigation of the globe was. Sir Ranulph Twisleton-Wykeham-Fiennes has become justly famous for his exploits and adventures, and latterly astonishing feats of fund-raising, but Ginny was always a much shyer figure, happiest as far from the limelight as possible. She was as devoted to Ran as he was to her, and in her own way was just as remarkable a figure – as determined, singular, thoughtful and kind a person as I have ever known. And she adored dogs.

She and Ran had taken their terrier Bothie with them round the world and then written a wonderful book about him (*Bothie the Polar Dog*). Bothie was singularly bad tempered and badly behaved, but adored by Ginny. While they were over-wintering at camp in Tuktoyaktuk before the journey on foot to the North Pole, Ginny took in an abandoned pup that was the offspring between a large Newfoundland bitch and a stray Labrador–husky cross. Such matings are not rare, but the local people never keep the pups as they are regarded as useless for work. The 'blackdogs' in the sledge teams are mostly a cross between Newfoundland and husky, and add brute strength to the team, even if they are somewhat short on the sheer hardiness and stamina of the huskies.

This squint-eyed orphaned pup stayed with Ginny at base camp as Ran set off to complete the circumnavigation of the globe by walking to the North Pole. She, along with the rest of the team who stayed at camp, survived a terrible fire, and was then sent back to the UK. The pup went into the obligatory six-month quarantine, while the Transglobe expedition made its perilous way to the top of the world and then back to London by boat.

The pup was called Blackdog. She was beautiful, wary, and had a terrifying stillness. I remember staying with Ran and Ginny on their Exmoor farm and getting up early to get a drink of water from the kitchen. Blackdog was lying across the stairs and as I descended she turned and looked at me with pale, unblinking eyes. It was as scary and threatening a moment as I have ever known with an animal. So I beat an exaggeratedly calm, conciliatory retreat, deciding that perhaps I was not so thirsty after all.

Ginny wanted to use Blackdog to re-establish what she believed to be the true Labrador – strong, thick-haired, with an extra layer of oily fur to resist water, and a far cry from the overbred examples that were beginning to become the norm by the mid-1980s. She crossed Blackdog with that year's gundog champion at Crufts, a large and handsome black Labrador.

Blackdog duly had a litter of ten pups, most pure black but a few marked with sandy streaks on their legs. Ginny called them St John's water dogs and saw them as the first examples of the new breed. She asked if we would be interested in taking one. Although, being Ginny, she managed to shyly enquire whether you would be at all interested and simultaneously manage to persuade you that of all the things in the world that you could do, taking one of these pups would be the sanest and most life-enhancing thing one could imagine.

When we went to choose, there were two brothers that were very alike and which seemed to operate as a pair. We already had Gretel and Eric, and Sarah was pregnant with our first child. Our jewellery business was consuming all of our time. We had builders extending the house. Clearly one more dog, let alone one more big dog, not to say one more big, potentially rather wild dog, and certainly not two more big wild dogs, were the very last thing we needed.

Hence the list.

Baffin was named after Baffin Island and Beaufort after the Beaufort Sea – both within the Arctic Circle and resonant of their mother's homeland.

As puppies they were inseparable, often sleeping stacked on top of each other, playing constantly, the two almost making one collective dog. Baffin was a little bigger, rangier and had a charming, open character. Beaufort was more feminine, reticent and even suspicious, but clever and extremely, even intensely responsive. He was more like his mother.

That winter was cold and the two pups loved the snow. I have an abiding memory of looking out of the upstairs window of our house in De Beauvoir Town and seeing them both curled up in the snow, having made their own little snow holes – just like the huskies I had seen curled up outside in a snowstorm on the shores of the frozen Hudson Bay.

I had always taken my dogs to work with me, Gretel lying quietly at my feet and Eric doing the rounds of our neighbours and employees. Until the two blackdogs were six months old or so, they came too. With hindsight this was chaotically barmy. But at the time it seemed sensible. After all, I couldn't leave them alone all day and I was besotted, so wholly unable to imagine that anyone might not think them an unmitigated joy . . .

But as they got older and bigger and more boisterous, this proved impractical. We built a large shed on to the side of the house – the most expensive kennel ever, according to Sarah – that had a deep freeze for the fish; although tripe, delivered by the hundredweight in one-pound blocks proved a more viable and very healthy alternative. I often wondered how and why the large-scale tripe delivery business started. For zoos? Packs of hounds? I never got round to asking. After taking them for a run each morning along the towpath of the Regent's Canal, down to and round Victoria Park, they spent the weekdays at home where we had made a large run for them. At weekends we would go to one of the great London parks and they would roam free, covering many miles.

These two large, loose-limbed but increasingly powerful dogs were a growing pleasure – affectionate, but with a self-reliance I had not come across in any other dog I had owned. If they liked you then they were warm and responsive, but if they did not know you or decided that you were not interesting, then they would simply ignore you. Baffin was open and generous and dominant, whereas Beaufort was sensitive and wary, but he loved with a passion. I never really thought of them separately. They were a pair. We were a team.

The blackdogs were happiest in water. Whether the Regent's Canal or the boating lake in Regent's Park in London, the sea in a gale or, memorably, a friend's swimming pool, the two dogs would hurl themselves into the water with a great leap so that they flew through the air and landed with a great splash before swimming powerfully, unfazed by any kind of wave or weather.

I remember one weekend when we were staying with Ran and Ginny on Exmoor to give moral and exemplar support. Ginny was due a visit from the head of the Kennel Club to discuss the acceptance of St John's water dogs as a recognised breed. An extremely large and doughty lady dressed in tweeds duly appeared, clearly very sceptical and regarding the whole set-up as dodgy. But tea was served and the dogs paraded out to her in turn, Huskey, Pollux, Baffin, Beaufort and Blackdog all behaving beautifully and looking magnificent. Although still reluctant to admit to the notion that the modern Labrador was less than perfect, she did thaw a little and offered a chink of light by saying that it would take at least six generations before the breed could be established. But the whole thing fell apart when she left and we all escorted her to her car. She opened the boot and let out her terrier, whereupon the pack of blackdogs fell upon it, and it was only saved by Ran diving in and hoisting it shoulder high by the scruff of its neck. She left as quickly as she could while the dogs fought each other in a rolling black maul.

Occasionally we would meet up with Ran and Ginny and take Blackdog, the three pups they had retained from the litter, and Bothie the terrier along with our four dogs for a walk. This mongrel pack charged around slightly alarmingly – somewhere between a screwball sledge team and an inner-city gang steaming a quiet row of shops. But mostly, when it was just me, I ran and walked with them early in the morning as it got light, with just a few fellow joggers about. The dogs and me free from the concrete claustrophobia of city life.

It was glorious, but I was aware it was also too restricted. There was a kind of vanity in owning these extraordinary dogs that was pandering more to my own canine needs than to their own.

That summer, with Adam, our firstborn, just a couple of

months old, we rented a cottage in Wales for a holiday. Four dogs, a newborn baby and two adults crammed into our car and drove off for a week in Welsh rain. By the second day the dogs were soaked, their bedding was soaked, we were soaked, and the car steamed gently with a mixture of damp and the rich aroma of wet dog. The cottage had no washing machine or dryer. It seemed a pretty good snapshot of our life.

When the pups were a year old, Gretel got cancer and died. It lessened the dog count but she was the gentlest, most biddable member of the pack.

In December the following year, our daughter was born. So we now had two children under eighteen months as well as two large, fully grown dogs, as well as a terrier given to starting a fight in an empty room. Oh, and a new shop in Knightsbridge, twenty members of staff and four collections a year to design and sell.

Then Baffin and Beaufort started to fight. Most of the time it was the usual rough and tumble of growing puppies, albeit of two very big, boisterous young male dogs. But increasingly this became real fighting, with nasty wounds that needed stitching. Leaving them together became an anxiety. Leaving them with the children was much worse. After one particularly fierce set-to, Sarah issued an ultimatum. We could not keep them. After much discussion we realised that it was neither of the two dogs that were at fault. They were doing what any males in a pack do, establishing dominance.

But the prospect of the children being caught in the cross-fire was beyond contemplation. Something had to be done. Soon. So we decided that one of them had to go. There was no question of putting either down. They were exceptional, almost unique creatures, just coming into their absolute prime. So I resolved to give one away to a suitable home.

Baffin was the better dog of the two by any measure and I loved him deeply. But Beaufort loved me almost obsessively and I knew that he would adapt less well – if at all – to anyone else. Parting with Baffin would break my heart, but keeping him would break Beaufort's.

So I placed an advert in *Country Life.* I did not ask for any money for him – just a good home.

A number of people replied, some extraordinary, some hopelessly unsuitable, but one immediately attracted me. It was from Elizabeth Forrest, who wrote me a letter saying she lived on an island off the west coast of Scotland which she shared with her husband Peter and an Irish wolfhound. The house had a Gertrude Jekyll garden. There would, she thought, be plenty of room for Baffin.

This turned out to be Little Cumbrae, an island two miles long and a mile wide, between Arran and the Ayrshire coast. I wrote back and arranged to drive up with Baffin in January

1988. We spent the night in a B&B in Skelmorlie and I walked him along the seafront, the wind cutting off the sea flapping his ears, with a sense of guilt, loss and resignation. Baffin did not mind at all. It was fun.

The next day we took the ferry from Largs to Cumbrae and drove down to Millport, where a little boat waited for us. Baffin stood in the prow, ears streaming in the wind. I had come with an absolute principle of not leaving him unless I was certain that he was in good hands, but already the sea and the hills suited him better than anything I could offer.

The boatman took us into a shallow inlet with a square tower like a castle keep on the waterfront and a large house set back from the water. Elizabeth Forrest waited on a small wooden pier with her Irish wolfhound. Baffin leapt off the boat, went straight up to the wolfhound; they circled and then threw themselves at each other. The hound had Baffin's leg and he had its head in his jaws. It didn't look too good for either of them but there was nothing Elizabeth and I – still shaking hands and politely greeting each other – could do. Gradually the intensity of each other's assault lessened; they released their grip and we dragged them apart. From that day onwards the two dogs carefully avoided confrontation, never fighting again, but never remaining in the same room together and keeping a good distance apart when outside.

With the dogs sorted, I looked around. It was a beautiful,

magnificent place. After lunch we took the two dogs for a walk on the hills behind the house. These covered nearly 700 acres of moorland across to coves and cliffs – and a lighthouse – facing northwest to the isles of Bute, Arran and Rothesay. It was romantic, wild and free.

That night I dined with Elizabeth and her partner Peter Kaye. Then in his seventies, Peter was an engineer and businessman who had founded Clyde Hover Ferries. When I asked him what his profession was, he said proudly that he was 'an industrialist' with an airline, a glass factory, and 'a few other businesses – all of which either made or did things.' A wise but angry man, despairing of the way that the world was turning, he had bought the island in 1960 and created a retreat from a world that he saw set to implode. The place was set up to withstand, if not disaster, then trouble in most forms. He had two generators, one solely as a back up. There were two boats and two full-time boatmen – one at the island and one at Cumbrae, and every time one set off the other would cross, so they were never stranded either on or off the island.

Although he was an unreconstructed capitalist, he saw trouble ahead because we – the British – were not making anything any more. 'People are making vast sums of money,' he said, 'passing bits of paper to each other and charging more and more with each transfer.' But sooner or later,' he added, 'the paper comes back round and you cannot pay for it. On top of which it is worth precisely nothing.' There was, he added ominously, mighty trouble coming.

In fact the mighty trouble had already come to our jewellery business, although we had not yet absorbed the extent of it, and we were to spend the next five years digging ourselves out of the pit that we were tumbling into. This was to mean winding down our business, laying off the staff, losing our own jobs, selling our home and almost all our possessions. But that evening in January 1988 I had no inkling of what lay ahead. The only thing on my mind was that my dog had found his new home.

I left him the next morning, standing on the pier with Elizabeth looking out to sea, as the little boat took me back for the long and lonely journey down to London.

Elizabeth kept in touch and assured me that Baffin had adapted to his new home. He would, she said, leap into the sea and swim with the seals. In April 1991 Sarah and I spent a week visiting gardens on the west coast of Scotland and went over to Little Cumbrae to see Baffin. He recognised me immediately and stood up with a huge paw placed on either of my shoulders, but it was clear that this was his home. I belonged to his past, and when we left he stood happily by Elizabeth's side, entirely her dog and living a wonderful life.

33. Beaufort

Beaufort blossomed once he was out of Baffin's considerable shadow. Whenever I threw a ball or stick for them, Beaufort had always got there first, whereupon Baffin always took it from him. Beaufort had always been the junior partner, the younger brother, always had something elegantly feminine about him compared to Baffin's bluff masculinity. He was a complex, sensitive and sometimes anxious soul. This made him much more interesting, but less accessible. In fact he loved deeply – mainly me, but also Sarah – and was happy as long as he was near one of us. He did not give or ask for much demonstrative affection.

It was enough for him to lie within a few yards, always watchful.

But my main memory of Beaufort, other than his fierce loyalty, was his athleticism. He ran like the wind and swam like an otter. He could leap a five-bar gate without breaking stride and take the hat off my head from a standing start without ruffling my hair. In his prime, which lasted from about two to seven, there was a purity of movement and purpose in all his actions that never failed to thrill.

In the summer of 1988 we left London in search of a larger garden and went to live in Herefordshire. For some time before we found Longmeadow we lived in a sprawling, very run-down house with acres of equally neglected land. Beaufort was like a paper flower opening in water. He throve. I would open the door in the morning and he would immediately shoot up the hillside; half an hour later he would return, tongue lolling, having toured his territory. After all the restrictions and privations of London it was pure, untrammelled freedom. It did not match Baffin's thousand-acre island, but he had free rein of thirty-three acres of Herefordshire hillside, with a wood, pond and complete safety, as the house was set up a long drive which in turn led off a small road that saw perhaps one car every couple of hours.

Sarah found an Inuit sledge in a junk shop in Bromyard,

and when it snowed we hitched him to it and he pulled the children up and, rather more alarmingly, down the slopes. I rather romantically thought that once in the traces, his Arctic genes might kick in, but I think he was merely playing along with a slightly baffling game.

I was making a garden there with almost manic intensity, and every step, every turf turned, was shadowed by Beaufort; then when I went indoors he came and lay by my side. While he did not object to anyone else, he at best tolerated and mainly ignored them. He realised that Sarah and the children were special and respected them accordingly, but he was completely a one-man dog. He was not jealous or possessive, just uninterested in anyone else.

For two years it was a kind of glorious but hopeless dream. While Beaufort and I were making a huge, elaborate garden, our jewellery business was disappearing down a voracious plughole. We knew it and could see it and had to deal with it daily – but in truth felt utterly powerless anywhere and anyhow except in the garden. So I buried myself in it.

Our world predictably crumbled and we had to sell up everything – really everything – and Beaufort came with us to Sarah's parents' house for six months, and then the rented rat-infested farmhouse (the rats scampered around inside the drawers of the kitchen units and if you opened them a tail would flick away to the back – not ideal).

On one particularly bleak February day, Eric the terrier was taken to the vet and put to sleep. His fighting and wandering had become uncontrollable and he spent almost all of his day tied up, sleeping in the hundred-pound car. He did not like it and we did not want it. He had had ten years of good, if zany, life, and clearly in those circumstances we could not cope. Nevertheless his death became the focus for a deep depression. I mourned Eric unreasonably and fell into bedridden, useless gloom. In fact this was the beginning of coming to grips with my chronic depression and, for the first time, asking for and receiving treatment, which was for me, and I suspect most men, the hardest step of all.

The following year was bleak. For the best part of six months I just did housework and made carved wooden bowls every day. Medication flattened and protected me. Throughout it all Beaufort was at my side, wise, constant and, perhaps most curative of all, in need of a long walk at least once a day.

During this year we found Longmeadow, which was then a ruined shell of a building with two acres of overgrown field. My mother had died and left me enough money to put down a deposit. It was uninhabitable, unmanageable but, at last, we were full of hope and there was a home and a garden to be made.

Just as Gretel had been a constant presence in the making of our London garden, so Beaufort was never more than a few yards from me as Longmeadow gradually became a garden. While the house was being made fit to live in, Beaufort and I would walk a mile or two across the fields from our rented house to work in the garden, clearing, planning, cutting back and raking up. He would watch me, tolerant but slightly bored, and then as a reward for his patience I would take him down to the river where he would leap off the steepest bank and belly-flop on to the water with obvious delight.

I remember being in the garden one day before we moved in, lost in plans and schemes when, looking up, I saw Beaufort a quarter of a mile away in a field far beyond the other side of the river. I called, he looked up, turned and ran straight back, swimming the river, hauling himself up the bank, covering the hundred yards to the garden's edge and leaping the barbed-wire fence with a foot to spare before shaking his wet coat all over me.

The river, although not large, would swell in flood and run with a dangerous rip. A man had died just at the end of our garden some years back, wading out into the flood on horseback, only to be swept from his mount and washed downstream. Beaufort loved the flooding and would swim and splash through it, then be swept away by the current in an alarming manner, although he would then turn around and patiently swim against it, slowly prevailing and making headway in a way that no human swimmer could ever have done.

34. The Coppice

For a few years the coppice was a piece of grass about sixty-five feet by sixty-five that lay between the Jewel Garden and the orchard. A ditch ran through it, which we filled with spoil, and I planted some Italian alders plus a couple of cherries and a few ash trees. Every one of those alders has since died, but the others have thrived; so it did claim the area for trees, albeit trees growing in and among grass.

In fact there were only two trees at Longmeadow until I started planting in spring 1993. One was a hawthorn – still there – in what is now the coppice, and the other was a large hazel outside the back yard. After a few years I noticed hazel seedlings popping up where squirrels had buried and then forgotten them. So I dug them up and after a few years had eighty little hazels all potted up.

I had grown up in the hazel/beech coppice countryside of north Hampshire and had grown to love the subtlety of those woods with their almost fluid pattern of growth and shade and the flowers and fauna that reacted to that shift. In fact I have always felt that the best gardens aspired to coppice and that the best woods have all the elements of the very best gardens.

So I decided to plant the hazels among the trees and create my own little coppice. That was nineteen years ago. The first few years were a real problem as the grass swamped the hazels. With hindsight I would have done better to have lifted all the turf and then mulched around the hazels with chippings until they were large enough to compete and then shade out grass and other weeds. I never considered, nor would do so now, using herbicide.

Those pathetically small seedlings have now become established hazel stools that I have coppiced – which is to say cut back to a stump, twice; the third coppice cycle is due in the winter of 2018/19. Each stool has up to twenty strong straight stems between ten and twenty feet tall, growing above a carpet of primroses, violets, wood anemones, narcissi and bluebells. The standard ashes and cherries are now large trees. It is my own little wood and I love it. It is a place filled with a gentle green light that comes sifting through the branches, and has a careless but precise beauty. It is filled with peace.

Which is why I chose it as the burial ground for my dogs.

Beaufort was the first to be buried there. His niece, Red, appeared on the scene when he was ten and seemed to re-energise him. He, the proudest and most aloof of dogs, tolerated her increasingly rough play with dignity and gentleness. The leaping into rivers got less, but he remained my shadow in the garden, rising increasingly heavily as I went to empty the wheelbarrow, but sticking with me.

But the years began to weigh heavily, and by the time he reached thirteen his body started to go awry. One evening he asked to go out rather early and I shushed him, immersed in some television programme. I then heard a noise and went into the hall to find him walking with a trail of pee – this proud, dignified dog cringing with shame, pissing himself.

His kidneys were failing and he ached and was weary. But to my eternal shame I did not take him to be put to sleep until I had finished the book I was working on. It was a completely selfish dereliction of duty as a pet owner. When you take on the life of a pet you take on its death too. That is the deal. But all books are absurdly demanding and all-consuming. They demand a level of commitment that leaves little room for much else. I had dreaded his death for a while, and in any event I did not think I could cope with the emotional trauma and meet the publisher's deadline – and there was huge pressure from them. So for an unnecessary few months he endured discomfort to make me feel better, still loyally trailing my every movement, slipping on the icy paths and heaving himself to his feet, a tired old boy, still dragging himself to lie uncomfortably at my feet as I wrote.

I finished the book (*Fork to Fork*) on a Friday afternoon, and at dawn the next morning got up and dug a deep grave in the coppice that I had planted just a couple of years before. It was March and the primroses and violets were flowering. The vet came at nine and we walked Beaufort slowly up the garden and he lay calmly on a sheet by the side of the grave. I stroked his head. Rest now old friend. Rest now.

The vet injected him. He gave one deep exhalation and slumped. We lowered him down in the sheet and I piled the soil back into the hole over him. We had a great slab of old red sandstone, too big and heavy for a path or step but too uneven for a seat, that I slowly manoeuvred up to the coppice and set over the grave. I planted more primroses and violets around the stone. The sun shone. It was a beautiful spring day but I felt as empty and fragile as an eggshell.

When your dog dies you are the broken child again, rattling with hurt.

But whereas I have never been back to Gretel's grave and have no wish to do so, I pass Beaufort's every day and often clean leaves and self-sown weeds from the stone. Now wood anemones, erythroniums and ragged robin jostle the gravestone in spring. It does not feel macabre in any way to know that he is there, literally and metaphorically still part of the garden.

35. The Cricket Pitch

The central path that cuts through the middle of the Cottage and the Jewel gardens goes on to divide the coppice into two sections and then arrives at the Cricket Pitch.

The name is not entirely fanciful, although one of the cricketers (me) would struggle to bowl a ball and the other (my son) has long lost interest in playing.

This top part of the garden was initially home to Charlie the foul-tempered Shetland pony. If nothing else – and there was nothing else – he acted as a grass cutter. Then, when he left us to act as an alibi for a publican's wife (it is a long and improbable story), I planted apple trees right across the top of the garden but honoured the alignment of the central path, which left a strip of grass that I mowed tight to continue the sense of the path. So when Adam, my eldest son, became very keen on cricket at school, I bought him a cricket net for his birthday and put it up in this avenue between the apples. For about three years we used it a lot although, like all fathers, I look back with regret and realise that I was always too busy to do so as much as I could or should have done. Then Adam lost his cricketing mojo and cricket was over.

The netting became a fruit cage (holes much too big and the blackbirds squeezed through them almost without breaking flight), and the sprung wicket is still, nearly twenty years later, stashed away in a shed. Maybe grandchildren will use them. But I had got used to the mown grass so I planted a hornbeam hedge either side and transplanted the apples so that the half of the orchard nearest the fields became denser. (This was a mistake and they have since had to be thinned.)

The hedges grew well and for some years we kept this regularly mown as lawn. We transplanted a horse chestnut in the bucket of a digger when we reconfigured the Mound and this became a focal point. Then we decided to reduce the mowing to a narrow strip and let the rest of the grass grow long. Gradually we underplanted it with crocus, fritillaries and the wild narcissi. Other than the central strip, the grass was left uncut till the bulb foliage had completely died back – about July – and then it was cut and gathered for compost, whereafter it returned to lawn again for the rest of the year. The latest development is to place large Italian pots along its length with topiarised box cones.

I look back over this progression in pictures and for a moment wonder why it was ever changed. But pictures reflect the best of anything. The perfect light or the day when all the flowers opened. The weeks and months of it not looking very good are never recorded. And gardens change. We have become used to visiting National Trust gardens and regarding them as fixed entities, like Chelsea Flower Show gardens, every detail held in suspension, knowing what we are likely to see and feeling cheated if it is not exactly as expected. But show gardens are dismantled after a week. No real garden can ever be like that. It grows and changes and rises and falls, and we change too. No moment is ever repeated – and that is what makes it so entrancing.

Nigel would have liked to have played cricket – hopeless batsman, not much of a bowler, but simply terrific in the outfield – but the cricketing days were long gone before he arrived on the scene. And he likes the cricket pitch not least because there are sheds and compost heaps and piles of wood up in that part of the garden, as well as the lure of the fields beyond, and all that adds up to squizzers – and nothing, not even a brand-new yellow tennis ball, is as good as hunting squizzers. Once upon a time squizzers referred directly to the squirrels that tantalised so cruelly in the branches above Nigel's poor, confused head. But quickly it became the generic word for anything furry that moved fast and demanded to be chased. The whisper of 'squiz' will send his ears up with his tail arching up over his back, every sinew strung taut.

Not that the hunt has been entirely successful. To date every dastardly squizzer remains on the loose. But we live in hope. Or at least Nigel does.

36. Poppy

I hired two transit vans for our mile-and-a-half move down the road into Longmeadow. What we did not immediately need was piled, floor to ceiling, into the sitting room, until there was just enough space to open the door and edge between the stacked furniture, scores of tea chests and hundreds of whisky cartons borrowed from Sarah's father. The cartons had my books in them, which had been packed for over a year and, in the absence of bookshelves, were to remain unpacked for fully another year. When her father died a couple of years ago, Sarah inherited his library – all packed neatly in the same whisky cartons, and which, like carefully folded used Christmas wrapping, we have neatly packed flat for the next move.

In truth, we did not have a lot. Most of it had been sold and what was left was either essential or worthless. My eighteen-year-old nephew Matthew came and helped me load and unload the vans, while Sarah managed the three small children and dogs. I had walked the pony over the day before and led him down the path to the front door, across the hall and out through the back door into the field behind and set him loose. As yet there was no garden of any kind for him to damage.

Sarah and myself, Matthew, the three children, and dogs Beaufort and Poppy sat round a door laid on two trestles in the kitchen and had our first meal in the house. Only the kitchen, two bedrooms and a bathroom were usable but it was, for the first time in nearly two years, our home.

Beaufort, as ever, lay at my feet, watchful. Poppy scampered around, still a puppy. Poppy was Eric's daughter, although we only discovered this after Eric's death. It seems that she was conceived on literally the last occasion Eric ran free, the morning before he was put down. Poppy's mother was a charming and rather hairy Jack Russell belonging to a traveller family who lived in a caravan in a field next door to the farmhouse in which we had spent the past fifteen months. About two months after Eric died we had a knock on the door. Our neighbour's bitch had just had a litter of eight pups. Eric had been observed in flagrante and, as far as they knew, no other dog had been near. As owners of the sire, would we like the pick of the litter? In light of all the problems of dealing with Eric's testosterone pugnaciousness, we decided to choose a bitch, and eight weeks later took possession of a tiny little puppy that the children immediately called Poppy.

Poppy was never beautiful, but she was sweet natured, with none of Eric's manic cussedness – at least not with humans. She had one half of her face tan and the other white, with a blaze that angled up her head and made her look constantly cock-eyed. Her coat was almost entirely white for the first few years of her life, but underlying dark spots and splodges became increasingly prominent as she got older.

She loved Beaufort and he was endlessly patient with her, allowing her to crawl all over him and gnaw away at various parts of his anatomy when she was a puppy and, as she got older, invariably carefully placing her bottom on his paws so she would be warm.

But she had a Jekyll and Hyde character. Indoors and in the garden she was gentle, meek and completely happy to potter around, as long as she was part of whatever was going on. If there was a fire she would lie in front of it, getting as close as possible and even lying in the warm ashes. If there was a meal she hoovered around expectantly but unaggressively. If there was a game she would play it. She responded but was completely happy not to instigate.

But once outside the domestic bounds, she became another animal completely. I would look out through the kitchen window and see Poppy's white tail in the field across the lane or even over on the other side of the river. She would apparently be lazing in the sun outside the front door, and then disappear, having slipped under the garden fence to quarter the fields and hedges, hunting with a focus and efficiency that you never saw in her domestic life.

When we took her for a walk she would systematically work the hedgerows for rabbits, disappearing after the first ten minutes and only rejoining us either at the very end of the walk or trotting home an hour or two later with a discernible swagger.

When we bought the house it was a ruin attached to a set of unused sheds, small barns and stables, all filled with a mixture of junk, old tools and unmucked-out animal manure. They were also filled with rats. Before we moved in I was working on the house when I came across a freshly killed rat under a floorboard in a bedroom. It was getting dark and the house had no electricity, so I left it alone meaning to explore where it had come in from in the morning when it was light. The next day I returned after breakfast and went up to move the carcass, and found that only the skin remained. The rest had been completely devoured overnight by other rats.

It took a few years to get the rats under control, and inevitably some would come into the buildings in autumn as the food supply in the fields and hedgerows dwindled. Poppy loved ratting and, at the slightest ratty whiff, she would stake it out, sometimes for days, until a rat, almost as big as Poppy, would be found dead as a post on the floor, with Poppy managing to be simultaneously both meek and triumphant.

She also hated most other dogs. Her father's genes rushed to the fore and the gentle little pet became an Amazonian warrior, outraged at the provocation of a passing neighbour with a perfectly innocent pet on a lead. If she could not get to the other dog directly, she would hurl herself at the fence or gate, ripping at it both in frustration and as a terrible warning of the punishment she intended to mete out when she got unfettered access. Then, when picked up and carried back indoors after profuse apologies, she would look as though butter would not melt in her mouth and play happily and completely safely with the children toddling around her.

When Beaufort died, Poppy became visibly depressed, and was never quite the same dog as before. She had been with him almost twenty-four hours a day for over six years since she was eight weeks old and she clearly grieved for him. The spring went out of her step. The meekness became slightly cowering and, although only eight, normally the prime of any terrier's life, she suddenly looked prematurely old. She increasingly seemed to fade into the background and become a shadow of her younger self.

Red had arrived on the scene for the last three years of Beaufort's life, and the three dogs seemed a happy unit, but clearly Red's presence, physically huge as it was, did not fill the gap that Beaufort left in Poppy's heart.

One thing that did not fade was her propensity to dig, often in the middle of mown grass or a flower or vegetable bed, causing horticultural havoc in the process. A mole would have her excavating tunnels along the length of a grass path and voles could happily keep her occupied destroying a large flower bed.

Poppy and I fell out over this a number of times. On one shameful occasion I found her digging a big hole in the middle of the cricket pitch, and in my rage I yelled at her. She ran off, terrified, while my rage quickly turned into guilt, knowing that I had done something terribly wrong. When I went to find her to apologise it was too late. She had disappeared.

This was around midday and by tea-time I was getting worried. I walked the fields calling, but there was no sign of her. It was summer and light till well after nine, but she still had not returned by the time it got properly dark. I took the car and drove around the lanes to see if I could find her, expecting to see her body as much as the live dog. But nothing at all. I walked the fields again at one in the morning with a torch and drove around again as soon as it got light. At eight a friend rang up and I mentioned Poppy's absence. She asked if we had rung the police.

'No – why would we?'

'Because if anyone picks up a stray they always ring the police,' she said. 'Our dogs often go missing and we always find them in the police dog pound.'

So I rang the police. Yes, a Jack Russell terrier had been reported, but no they did not have it. It was at the Monkland Kennels. These are half a mile away from us as the crow flies, and nearly four miles by road, so I rushed round there. Poppy was having breakfast. She seemed perfectly happy and – to rub salt into my already stinging guilt – was delighted to see me. It turned out that after my outburst she ran off across the fields and found her way to the nearest pub – which is next door to the kennels. She spent the evening there being fed titbits by drinkers but, as it became apparent that she did not belong to anyone and no one had seen her around before, she was deposited in the kennels for safe-keeping.

From then on, if none of us could immediately find Poppy and asked where she was, the answer would always be, 'She's gone down the pub.'

When Poppy was thirteen she started to have fits. She would be trotting along on a walk and then suddenly keel over and her legs would twitch and tread empty air before she lay completely motionless as though dead. When you went up to her, her eyes would be wide open and she would froth at the mouth. Then, after perhaps thirty seconds, she would come to, groggily get to her feet and walk on, clearly dazed. It was frightening, but the vet assured us that it was not unusual; it was likely to indicate a kidney problem but that in any event nothing could be done.

Thirteen years to the day that we moved into the house, I came downstairs to find Poppy stretched out in her bed – as though she had fitted – but clearly dead. I carried her in a cardboard box to the potting shed so the children should not see her.

I buried her in a little grave in the coppice as close as possible to Beaufort, where she had always most liked to lie.

37. The Writing Garden

For quite a few years the writing garden just had long grass – the original meadow – and four apple trees ('Rosemary Russet', 'James Grieve', 'Herefordshire Beefing' and 'Lane's Prince Albert') that were part of the orchard. On one side was the reverse of the hornbeam hedge flanking the cricket pitch, and on the other a mown path. One end opened into the coppice and the other butted on to a ploughed field. Then I planted hedges to fully enclose it and, finally, when I was recovering from an illness a few years ago, my son converted a shed he had built so that I could go and write there on fine days.

It became one of my favourite places, especially in spring when the grass was filled with billowing cow parsley and the apple trees were in blossom. The only 'gardening' I did there was to keep a curving path mown to the door of the shed. I deliberately kept mobile phones and computers away from there, and would work using a fountain pen or my father's old typewriter, freeing myself from the tyranny of modern communications.

However, the truth is that after the cow parsley died down – round the beginning of June – and if bad weather flattened the long grass before it reached its mature best around the end of June, and if the moles did their worst all winter, and if the weather was largely wet and cold, then its pleasures were very fleeting and the hut remained largely unvisited.

So a few years ago we took up all the grass. The curving mown path was replaced by bricks (lovely old ones that had been the floor of an old outhouse) and everything else dug for the first time for hundreds of years, if ever, so the entire garden was just path and border. The apple trees remained but now stood in the middle of the borders and supported roses and clematis.

Nigel trots down this new path of old bricks, not least because in the writing hut itself is an old cricket bat (bought from Jack Hobbs sports shop at the Angel in 1981 and still perfectly serviceable) and chasing a tennis ball whacked by a cricket bat across a grassy field combines all the best elements of cricket, tennis and just galloping about. Come to think of it, Nigel is very good about paths and borders. He very rarely strays from the path and wanders heavy-footed into a border, unless it is to retrieve a mis-thrown ball. But it is as though he actively likes them, and his step gains an extra spring when he takes to one. Perhaps it is because paths mean going somewhere, and going somewhere is nearly always interesting, even though it might turn out just to be there as opposed to here.

Perhaps it is because flowers do not really interest him and he is moving on past them as quickly as possible. The old long grass would have had more interesting scents.

But they interest me. I have snowdrops, white crocus, the creamy narcissus 'Thalia', the pink and white tulip 'Lady Jane', tiarella 'Iron Butterfly', *Dicentra spectabilis* 'Alba', and the marvellous sweet woodruff *Galium odoratum*, followed by a display of the magnificent white allium 'Mount Everest' and white camassias.

The trick is to suggest and capture that lightness of touch with umbellifers like the two Ammis, *majus* and *visnaga*, seseli, fennel and *Orlaya grandiflora* so that it floats over and among the rest of the planting, which in turn can be more varied and various, including climbing roses like

'Wedding Day' and 'Sander's White Rambler' as well as shrub roses *Rosa rugosa* 'Alba', *Rosa* 'Madame Legras de Saint Germain' and *R.* 'Madame Plantier'. There are the clematis 'Alba Luxurians', *C. flammula* and *C. fargesioides* 'Summer Snow' (also known as 'Paul Farges'), white foxgloves, *Nicotiana sylvestris*, the sweet white rocket *Hesperis matronalis* var. *albiflora* 'Alba Plena', *Dicentra spectabilis* 'Alba', white sweet peas, white cosmos 'Purity' and the frothy sea kale, *Crambe cordifolia*. The intention is that all this retains the constant freshness of the hundred shades of green foliage and all white flowers.

However, the real secret of setting off white flowers to their best advantage is their relationship to green. In fact a so-called 'white' garden is really a green garden with touches of white.

Whether because of this carefully coordinated colour theme, or just that he can see down the garden from there, Nigel likes the writing garden, and I often find him lying on the cool bricks surrounded by white flowers that make his coat look more russet than ever.

38. The Orchard

Nigel loves the orchard for two special reasons. The first is the apples that it produces, which double up as scrumptious snacks as well as edible balls, and the second is that it leads to the fields beyond, which hold the licence to roam and gallop in great arcing wheels and to dive into the river and swim. In fact to go for a walk with arcing wheels, etc., have a bracing swim and then come back and munch on two or three apples constitutes an extremely successful afternoon.

It is only an orchard because I made it so. Like the rest of Longmeadow it was a field, and I did not begin planting the apple trees until the autumn of 1997, completing it the following spring.

I chose the trees – all thirty-seven different varieties, some doubled – as a mixture of a practical supply of favoured food, such as 'Bramley's Seedling', 'Newton Wonder', 'Jupiter' and 'Ribston Pippin'. Others were locally bred or raised so seemed appropriate, including 'Tillington Court', 'Madresfield Court', 'Herefordshire Pearmain' and 'Stoke Edith Pippin'. Yet others, like 'Crimson Queening' and 'Hambledon Deux Ans' just attracted me by their names.

In my mind I was making a great billowing orchard of mature standards, whose branches would meet in a flowering, fruity canopy and whose shade would protect sheep that gently nibbled the grass to a sward. In practice a bundle arrived with each 'tree' no bigger than a modest bamboo cane. However, they were all on standard or semi-standard stock, and I planted them all six yards apart. You could only really tell where they were by the stakes that supported them.

After about five years I moved quite a few to make room for more garden, and planted these in the gaps, closing the spaces. They were all still so small that it hardly seemed to matter, but fifteen years on I have come to regret the decision and have removed quite a few to allow the remaining ones space to grow and spread. The moral of the story is 'have faith and patience'. Trees grow.

And now they have grown, the orchard has that lovely sense of a tree-garden that all the best orchards – and only orchards – have. They make beautiful blossoming trees but their fecundity is a vital part of the magic. Ask Nigel.

Gradually the wild daffodil *Narcissus pseudonarcissus* has spread, and in fifty years' time will carpet every inch under the trees. Chickens scratch and career about and we now have a couple of beehives at the end of the orchard. We have kept orphaned lambs in there, a bolshie ram, and a few years ago fattened three pigs on the windfalls. All the animals seemed at home, although Nigel didn't quite know what to make of the pigs. In truth he was a little scared of them.

The really dramatic change to the orchard has just come about recently. The fences that kept the various animals in – and Nigel out – have been removed and large expanses of the grass have been dug up to make what we now call the Orchard Beds.

These fall into two sections: one is a pair of matching borders that flank the path leading to the water meadows, planted to pick up the pinks and whites of the apple blossom. So far I have planted a loose structure of about twenty species of roses, quite a few peonies, hydrangeas, a couple of amelanchiers, and then filled that out with a lot of annuals and about twenty large plants of the dahlia 'Rothesay Reveller', which flowered profusely from July through to November. It is early days and will take a few years for the borders to fill out and establish their identity.

The other area is a huge rectangular bed – bigger than our entire garden in London – that has four apple trees and a very large pear, and so is essentially a woodland border filled with plants that thrive in light shade, such as ferns, foxgloves, tiarella, tellima, primulas, meconopsis, hellebores and honeysuckle climbing into the apples with more roses.

Although some of this is driven by a desire to satisfy television's endless hunger for new material, it is also fun, and any excuse to grow more of our favourite plants is eagerly taken.

~

September delivers Nigel's favourite harvest from the garden. A bout of blustery wind will bring down the first windfalls in the Orchard, and Nigel will head purposefully up to the top of the garden, nose through the day's offerings and devour them with relish, the greener and more unripe the better.

Nigel likes lying in the dappled coolness of the blossom, but loves, really truly loves, the windfall apples. In his first year the windfalls came when he was three or four months old, and at first we could not understand why he, who by then was housetrained and reliably discreet and regular in his habits, developed an upset tummy that left green dog-pats around the garden, as though a herd of incontinent cattle had wandered through. Then we realised that he was eating a dozen or so unripe apples a day and his puppy digestive system was understandably rebelling at this. Not that he seemed to mind in the slightest, and the repercussions have never put him off this seasonal treat. Nigel adores a windfall apple.

Rather than select a fruit from the ground and take it to eat in peace, he always stays standing above the chosen fruit and munches it in situ. But in order to bite the shiny skin he has to use his molars, so is forced to turn his head sideways to get a purchase on the fruit. As the apple gets eaten and thus smaller and smaller, his head twists more and more until his shoulder is practically on the ground and his body twisted at right angles. It cannot be comfy but he never changes his method.

We have over forty apple trees at Longmeadow that carry an awful lot of fruit. In fact, far more fruit than we can ever store, even though we eat apples daily throughout the autumn and winter and some will keep until May. This means that there are more windfalls than even Nigel can munch his way through between late August and midwinter – by which time the visiting fieldfares and redwings descend on the orchard in flocks to eat what Nigel has left behind.

But an apple is never just a delicious bite of forbidden fruit for Nigel. It has the great added bonus of looking to all intents and purposes like a slightly strangely (wrong) coloured tennis ball that can be thrown, chased, carried and endlessly plonked in a wheelbarrow or trug, followed by a foot-shuffling impatient bark for it to be thrown – again.

His devotion to an individual apple can last for days, despite it becoming progressively chewed, bashed and pulpy as a result of being hurled against trees and hedges and Nigel taking sneaky little bites from it. A ball you can eat surpasses all other dreams.

I have never quite worked out his favourite variety of apple. He seems to like the smaller ones to play with – so apples like 'Newton Wonder', 'Bramley's Seedling' or the enormous 'Glory of England' – and preferably with a touch of red in their colour, such as 'Spartan', 'Jupiter', 'Gala' or 'Ribston Pippin'.

However, the colour cannot be part of this choice, as dogs cannot see the red end of the colour spectrum clearly. They have one less cone than we do so, although they clearly distinguish blue and yellow, they cannot tell red or green apart and red, purple, orange and green appear as shades of green or blue – as for many colour-blind humans. Our reds are a muddy greeny-brown to dogs, so all apples will appear a lighter or darker shade of yellowy green. This suggests that the red in the colour is a symptom of the stimulus rather than the deciding factor itself.

In fact red apples are sweeter and have more sugar than green ones, and it is probably this that Nigel is attracted to. Certainly he loves 'Strawberry Pippin', which not only has red skin but pink, ultra-sweet flesh, and the late ripening 'Spartan', which develops a deep red, almost purple skin that burnishes to a chocolate colour when stored and is very sweet. It is also one of the last to fall and the last to be eaten by the birds, staying edible on the ground for dogs and humans well into the New Year.

39. The Mound

The third of the parallel paths that run the length of the garden begins at the end of the Lime Walk and forms a long section where the Damp Garden leads to the grass borders (having crossed the Long Walk) and from the grass borders up steps on to the Mound.

The Mound has accumulated for over twenty years, from the spoil of making a house and garden, and was where we had our bonfire until it had become a really sizeable heap. We then hired a digger, and in a day had shaped it from a random dump to a contoured pillow of earth. For some years this was smoothly mown grass where the children could

237

sprawl and look at the clouds and where we could watch the midsummer sun sinking below the tree line on one side and the shadows stretching over the garden below us on the other. But over the past five years this has been elaborated into a separate little garden of its own, made up of two terraces with a retaining wall and two sets of steps.

The lower level, which is paved, gets the full summer sun, and we fill it with pots of citrus, agapanthus, lilies and salvias around seats and a table; it makes the perfect place for an evening drink. The higher level is essentially one large border with a narrow brick path leading to a small bricked square just large enough for a circular table and four chairs. The plan has always been to construct a small building there – but somehow we have never quite agreed on how it should be and, following the basic garden rule that everyone has a veto, we wait until everyone agrees on what is to be done. It means that some parts of the garden evolve very slowly, but there is usually a good reason for this and there is no hurry. It has taken twenty-five years for the Mound to take the shape that it has now, so it can wait a few years more to get exactly the right structure on top of it.

It is essentially a scented garden and surrounded by espalier pears like battlements. The choice of plants is driven by their fragrance, and especially those that release their scent in the evening, which is when we go and sit there as the light falls.

So we have lavender, wallflowers, night-scented stock, *Nicotiana sylvestris*, verbena, honeysuckle and evening primrose (which is one of those welcome weeds that pops up all over Longmeadow). On the lower terrace, in pots, we have lilies, citrus, the chocolate-scented *Cosmos atrosanguineus* and lots of scented-leafed pelargoniums such as *Pelargonium graveolens*, *P. tomentosum* and *P.* 'Lady Plymouth', whose leaves I cannot resist gently pinching in passing to release their musky scent.

Longmeadow is flat, so the Mound, like the Elizabethan 'mounts', becomes a viewing platform, and the only spot in the garden, short of shinning up a tree, where you can look down and survey the rest of the garden around you. In fact it faces the coppice, so in summer especially, that creates a green wall which does not offer much view although provides complete privacy in this exposed place. To the east is the Jewel Garden, the grass borders and the Cottage Garden, and to the west the orchard and the setting summer sun.

To the north are open fields, water meadows. When they flood, the first place Nigel goes to is the Mound, our one high spot. There he looks out over the river and the lake that has appeared where the water meadows used to be, over the top of the hedges on to the water meadows and river, like a captain on his deck surveying the grassy high seas.

40. The Grass Borders

Apath takes you down a set of steps on the side of the Mound into the grass borders. These used to be part of the Jewel Garden, but the decision to group all the grasses together to make one grass garden was an aesthetic one. It needed no reshaping or landscaping, just some editing of plants that we already had, with a few more added.

It meant that the Jewel Garden would no longer include grasses, which it had done from its inception, and that the four large borders that now contained them would be much, much less labour intensive as a result. In truth, had we not begun to film at Longmeadow, I suspect that the whole of the Jewel Garden would have been given over to grasses.

The companion plants are chosen for their vertical form and height rather than colour, such as cardoons, onopordums, heleniums, rudbeckias, cirsiums, *Angelica gigas*, *Knautia macedonica*, coreopsis, *Helianthus salicifolius*, inula, macleaya, self-sown but encouraged thalictrum, *Verbena bonariensis*, asters, mulleins, tree dahlias, kniphofias and masses of bronze fennel. The result is a flowing, swaying dance of rich but subtle colour.

The four large beds surround a paved area with four limes planted in each corner, pleached to form a sheltering cube, and it is here that Nigel often lies, his coat blending with the tawny and russet shades of the grasses as they bleach into autumn, and surveys the garden.

No other piece of the garden changes so much over the seasons. In early spring, after all the dead growth has been removed and the lime cube cut right back to its framework, it is pretty bare, almost empty. There is something protestant and northern about grasses – at their best pared down, simple and very stylish, and at their worst unimaginative and dull. Ours, of course, are never dull . . .

Even so, they are unarguably slow to get going in our cold wet soil and do not really start to reappear until May. The allium 'Purple Sensation' and tulip 'Ballerina' still appear as gaudy ghosts from their Jewel Garden past: irreverent, out of place and very welcome.

By mid-June the new green growth of the grasses has a lusciousness to it. The cardoon are all glaucous foliage, spilling over itself with leaf, and the stipa flower heads catch the late midsummer light like flaming brands.

But by midsummer the grasses act as an understorey to the knautias, verbenas, eremurus, mulleins, cardoons and onopordums, biding their time until they really take over in late summer and on into autumn, when the combination of their colours, sheer scale and lovely arcing stems are quite the best thing in the whole garden.

October brings an amazing richness of colour, from the deep plum of the flower heads of *Miscanthus sinensis* 'Malepartus', to the gold of the fading foliage of all the grasses. At this point the grasses are, to my mind, the best and richest players in the garden.

Winter becomes them well, burnished with frost; the stems, especially of the various miscanthuses, strong enough to withstand rain and wind – which is just as well, given the winter weather we have had for the past few years.

Like so much in this garden, I cannot see only the current flowering of the grasses, whatever the season. It is rich with all the changes just beneath its skin. Before it was the bottom bit of the Jewel Garden, it used to be four more vegetable beds, and before *that* it was where we kept the chickens, guinea fowl and ducks and had a willow circle for the children – and, like everything else, before that it was part of one open, empty field.

All these changes in use were evolutionary, inasmuch as it felt as though we were working our way into the garden we wanted and it needed trial and error and even temporary occupancy (i.e. the veg) in order to make the right decisions. Then, opportunity and circumstance find the garden you want at that time. I still feel completely relaxed about the prospect of it all changing again at some future date. Nothing is so precious or fixed that it could not be wholly refashioned almost overnight.

I regard the planting in areas of the garden like decorating a room. Even if you radically change their use, the room stays in the same place. So I would be loath to alter the path that divides the grass borders from the Jewel Garden because it is so full of memory and quirky detail. The exact crossing between the two is always the first part of the garden to freeze. I have often walked out on a cold night and suddenly felt the grass crunch beneath my feet at that intersection. I am not sure why – it is not the lowest part of the garden – but it is invariably the case.

It is also the point where Poppy often used to lie and where Red, the second of the blackdogs we had here, always used to bring a trophy stick and chew it happily to splinters.

Red was, above all, the family dog. The dog my children grew up with, the dog that was here in the critical ten years when the garden went from an early gesture of hope to something like a mature place.

In many ways – other than that she was black, a girl and much bigger – she was very similar to Nigel, in that she was as loyal and gentle as the day was long, yet perhaps not the sharpest knife in the box, and that we all adored her.

41. Red

J ust before Christmas in 1995, ten years after we got Baffin
and Beaufort, Sarah and I drove to Suffolk to choose a
new dog.

Big dogs rarely live long. Gretel had been ten. Baffin had
died a year before on his Scottish fastness, aged nine, which
was early but not tragically so, having lived an almost perfect
life. Beaufort was now slowing down noticeably and we wanted
him to overlap, at least for a few years, with any new dog.

Having had large male dogs I was now determined to get
a bitch – in fact I vowed never to have another male dog
again (Nigel put paid to that). Bitches leave brown marks on

lawns when they pee but dogs, and especially large dogs, can cock a leg and spray hedges, topiary, borders and pots, causing horticultural havoc.

This new pup was from a litter fathered by Baffin and Beaufort's brother, crossed with a Newfoundland. When we got there the pups all had a different colour ribbon round their necks to identify them. There were only two bitches, but one immediately seemed right. She was fluffy, almost spherical, and had a slightly goofy charm. In this she was never to change. Around her neck was a red ribbon, so we called her Red.

Although she was nominally my dog, unlike Beaufort she seemed to give her heart to all the family equally. The children adored her and she was supremely patient and gentle with them. From the first she was always overgrown, the child in the class too big for the desk, clumsy but careful, endlessly good-natured, but sensitive to admonition. If Beaufort always had a sliver of his mother's untameable Arctic soul within him, Red had an extra-large portion of ice cream.

Her eyes were small at the best of times, and became almost wholly buried in black hairy wrinkles when you were cross with her. As this made her look adorable, it had two effects. The first was to stop being cross almost instantly, and the second, I am ashamed to say, meant that we would pretend to be cross just to get her to wrinkle her brow – and then make a big fuss, which meant she was happy but confused.

But as that was pretty much her constant state of mind, it did not seem to matter too much.

She gave Beaufort a new lease of life and he became energised by her, tolerating the inevitable puppy play that went too far and on for too long. The rather aloof loner became benign and clubbable and, as Red grew into a young dog – albeit already bigger than him by the time she was eight months old – the pair of them ran and chased balls together and swam side by side with easy familiarity.

Red shared with Nigel his deep and unshakeable passion for yellow tennis balls. But, unlike him, who loves them in sequence, Red loved them in parallel. One never satisfied. She would walk around carrying two, and occasionally three, in her mouth, with a look of total and utter bliss, like a child cramming its mouth with sweets before they could be taken from her.

She quickly cottoned on that I had made a garden consisting of runways like bowling alleys and assumed that these existed solely for her entertainment. When I was outside, my only role in life was to throw two balls simultaneously so she could then make a cavalry charge after them, picking up the first without stopping and then swooping on the second to join it in her mouth. More often than not, the collateral damage to the garden was considerable, with 120 pounds of skidding dog prepared to crash through a brick wall to collect her rightful tennis ball – let alone box hedging, dahlias, pots, grasses, or any of a hundred permutations of plants. In fact, I started to make more low woven hazel fences and plant more box edging solely to protect the borders from Red's uncontrollable retrieving.

The retriever in her meant that she would nearly always find whatever it was she was looking for and bring it back to where she started – although she would only let me have it as and when she wanted it thrown again. The process was always for her and never, as it usually is with Nigel, teamwork with me. Like Nigel she was acutely gun-shy, so balls and sticks were the summit of her ambition. In fact it was obvious that this was the summit of all her desires, aspirations and skills. To suggest otherwise was just silly . . .

For such a big dog Red was a dainty eater. She would pluck and nibble at her food, always finishing it eventually but often having two or three sessions at it. Red greeted the arrival of food with great enthusiasm, but I think she never really mastered the mechanics of eating out of a bowl very well, finding managing tongue, teeth and food in the mouth at the same time all a bit tricky. What Red really loved was her bedtime biscuit. I had found a supply of large square biscuits, each one the size of a small book, much like an old-fashioned ship's biscuit – and as hard. Red would take it gently from me with a look of exhilarated gratitude and retire to her bed and eat it very slowly, one massive paw pinning it down so that no one could come and take it from her.

But she was an expert sleeper. Indeed, she devoted by far the largest part of her life to it, sleeping around twenty hours of every day if you add in all the quick naps and snoozes that she fitted into her busy sleep schedule. She was a generous sleeper, very happy for any one, or at times all three, of the children, one of the cats and certainly any of our other dogs, to use her as a pillow and sleep with her.

Red died on 7 May 2006. It was a Saturday. She had seemed to be fine, although we all noticed that occasionally on a walk she would stop and lie down – but we put this down to laziness and, anyway, it was never for long, and when she resumed it was with plenty of enthusiasm. On the Thursday morning I went off to Berryfields just outside Stratford-upon-Avon to film an edition of *Gardeners' World*. She was sleepy but ate her breakfast. When I came home that night the house was empty. I came into the darkened hall and Red lay at the far end. For the previous eleven years, without fail, she had greeted me by running up and placing her paws on either shoulder. This time she looked at me but did not get up and in that instant I knew she was terribly ill.

The next morning I took her to the vet first thing. He said her heart was going to pack up any moment. He could keep her and put her down now, or she could lie quietly at home and he would come to our house over the weekend. I had to go off and finish filming *Gardeners' World*, so we agreed he would come the next day.

The Saturday was a perfect, ideal English May morning. I let Red out and left her for a moment. When I returned she had gone. Vanished. This was a dog that could scarcely walk. I eventually found her at the end of the garden, in the coppice, lying beneath the cherry tree, just next to Beaufort's grave. The white blossom fell around her. It must have taken her all her strength to walk there. She lay there all morning and the vet came and injected her where she lay. I buried her next to Beaufort and Poppy. She was a huge dog and the ground was hard. I embarrassed my children by weeping in front of the vet. I loved her. We all did.

42. The Dry, Courtyard and Walled Gardens

The garden in front of the house is much smaller than the plot out at the back and divided into four distinct areas. That division is largely created by the curving stone wall that originally partitioned the working farmyard from the garden of the farmhouse.

We have slightly rejigged and extended the wall to create an area on one side which for many years was the tarmacked yard where all building materials were for the ongoing – and very slow – process of restoring the house.

This is now the Dry Garden, and a favourite spot for Nigel

on filming days, because this is where the mess room for the film crew is, and Nigel always charges in on a filming day, barking a greeting at familiar faces and introducing himself to anyone new, all in delighted high spirits. One of the main attractions of the mess room is that this is where they have lunch and, while he is not pushy about these things, when it comes to crew lunch or indeed the odd snack, Nigel is very happy to oblige should they feel that they need his assistance.

The planting of the Dry Garden was entirely predicated by the almost total absence of soil. Once the tarmac was lifted we dug out a shallow tray in the red sandstone and filled it with a mixture of topsoil and compost. The sandstone drains very well and roots find their way into it, so really quite top-heavy plants like cardoons and giant verbascum gain enough anchorage to support themselves. Nevertheless we have chosen plants that thrive in very dry, poor conditions. However, it is south-facing and backed by heat-retaining walls, as well as fairly sheltered from the prevailing west wind. In practice, drought is never a problem, as rain has always recently been or is on its way, and we have never watered there – or indeed any other border in the garden.

The path through the Dry Garden passes through a pair of doors into our private area where we do not film.

Speaking as a willing member of them, I can faithfully report that all film crews are invariably cheerful, friendly, considerate and as unintrusive as possible. But . . . I remember advice when I started in television nearly thirty years ago, from the man who was my first agent and who had spent a lifetime in television and showbiz. 'Never let a circus or a film crew in your house, old boy,' he said. 'But if you have to choose, opt for the circus. They will make less mess.' In short, given that the crew are with us thirty weeks of the year, the family need somewhere that is truly private as and when they want to use it, without the risk of being in the back of shot or making a noise.

The little stone-flagged courtyard has a door into the house and leads to the walled garden and the front garden with the clipped yew cones.

The walled garden was the first piece of Longmeadow to be made although, when we arrived in 1991, it was, like the rest of the site, a rubble-strewn overgrown dumping ground. I planted a yew hedge parallel to the long side of the wall to enclose the area, and this grew quickly and well to make the perfect green wall. It is a mistake to be timid of planting yew in the belief it grows too slowly. Given good drainage and good soil, it will make a foot a year of healthy growth, which can then be clipped to make the perfect backdrop for a border as well as providing privacy and structure.

The walled garden has seen a number of changes, from the open grassy space with heaps of buried rubble, to its original layout of four large beds with woven hazel edges and further borders round the wall. This was where we planted all the plants that we had brought with us while the remainder of Longmeadow was making the slow transition from rough field to cultivated ground to a space. Then there was a shift to a place where the family could relax and play, with a small lawn to accommodate the children's paddling pool and then trampoline as they grew up.

This is the family retreat, where we often sit and eat or read, surrounded by my favourite old roses and herbaceous perennials as well as lots of pots filled with lavender and scented-leafed pelargoniums, and where, over the years, the children have had a paddling pool and trampoline, and where now Nigel stretches out and takes in the sun while remaining – as ever – the centre of attention.

43. Nellie

Nellie arrived on a November evening.

My oldest son had suggested that we get another dog so that by the time Nigel got old it would be a mature and integrated part of the household. It was succession planning again. The overlap would rejuvenate him and educate and integrate the puppy. We talked around and about this for months without making any effort to do anything about it. But should it eventually happen, I was sure of one thing: she would not be a he. No dog has ever been easier or better behaved than Nigel, but nevertheless he can be headstrong and a handful when with other male dogs.

Then I got a call from my son saying he was going up to Lincolnshire next week to collect 'my' new dog. And so Nell appeared.

I don't know what I had expected. A feminine version of Nigel, I think. But from the first minute she was Not-Nigel. Although all golden retriever puppies look identical and she has exactly the same body language – sitting, for example, in the same ultra-polite way when the prospect of food is on offer, as though she will get more for good behaviour – everything about her character is unlike his.

She is curious about everything and has none of Nigel's passivity – and might have much less of his ability to soak up attention. She is very much a Girl whereas Nigel is a Bloke.

For the first week or so Nigel was wary to the point of ignoring her. Inevitably a small puppy – particularly a very cute small puppy – is going to be the centre of attention. But not Nigel's. He disdainfully ignored her at first, preferring to leave the room rather than respond to her advances.

But gradually she won him over. He did not respond directly, but let her clamber all over him. Nell barked and yipped at him, frustrated by his lack of playfulness, and crept into his affections bit by bit. Soon Nigel became her plaything, like a vast teddy bear; he was endlessly tolerant even when she was clearly hurting him.

She would attack again and again, clinging on to any part

she could reach, with Nigel gently deflecting her, usually by rolling his head or bottom away to leave the puppy rolling on top of herself. And then she would suddenly collapse and become exhausted and we would stroke her for about a minute and she would be out like a light.

I remember Beaufort, normally pretty intolerant and sparing with his time and attention, being the same with Poppy and again with Red. It must be something that is wired into adult dogs. I wonder at what point the puppy tolerance goes and they get treated as another, possibly competitive adult. Not until twelve months, I think.

Nell grew daily, changed weekly and, by the time you read this, will be an adult dog creating her own life as part of our lives, her own world as part of this garden. Where she is clever, Nigel is wise. She is always up to mischief whereas he has always been a goody two-shoes. Nigel has never stolen a piece of food in his life (apart from peas), but Nell will jump on the table and eat whatever is there if you leave the room for a minute. Nigel is self-contained and greets any given situation with a world-weary but patient acceptance, whereas Nell quickly gets bored and looks for suitable entertainment.

Training Nigel was easy because he wanted to please. Training Nellie has been both easier and more demanding because she wants to do the work with an intensity and a hunger that Nigel only shares when a yellow ball is involved.

Nell retrieves with the sharpness of a sheepdog at work, whereas if you throw something for Nigel he goes and fetches it because he is a thoroughly decent chap.

But Nellie is good for him. She has sharpened him up. And while she is youth nipping at his heels, he is not yet ready to give up the reins. There is life in the old dog yet.

44. Ageing

Nigel is now eight. He is still very fit, loves going for long walks in the Welsh hills in any weather, chases rabbits and squizzers with enthusiasm, can jump well, swim, and will chase after any ball or object thrown for him. For two or three hours he can hold his own with any dog of any age.

But he is definitely slowing down.

He is later in the mornings and earlier in the evenings. Much of his day is spent dozing in the sun if it is there to be dozed in, and in the warmth of the kitchen if it is not. His ways are fixed and you can sense a slight irritability if a new regime is imposed upon him. I have to say that I am completely in tune with this. I guess we are growing older together.

His muzzle has faded and is distinctly grey, his nose has lost its black sheen and is a slightly splodgy pink; his eyes are a little rheumy and hollow. In short, he is starting to look old.

He is still astonishingly handsome, and still has a prance in his step when setting off outside. But when he comes in there is a weariness in him that never showed before. He sleeps deeply and long, shifting and groaning as he finds a new comfy position. Perhaps he has just learnt the art of pacing himself.

When Nigel hurt his back, Noel Fitzpatrick warned me that it might well come back to haunt him as he got older, and the important thing was to keep him fit and strong but not to strain him in any way. But one of the joys of Nigel has always been his exceptional athleticism. Were he to become a stiffly plodding, slightly rotund old boy then perhaps not enough of him would remain.

None of this is to say that Nigel does not have years of active life ahead. As good a measure as any are the triggers that a dog responds to when it thinks it is going for a walk. These are sometimes subtle – a particular key being unhooked that unlocks a gate to a park, or a certain coat – but for Nigel the certain sign is putting on outdoor shoes. In winter that invariably means wellies, and in summer lace-up boots. This means either a walk or gardening, and both mean outdoors, and that is fine by him. As I put on my wellies he is frantically looking for the right ball to carry outside – and can't leave the house without it. That eagerness is not remotely diminished yet. The day Nigel stops caring about a tennis ball is the day I will be really worried.

Dogs have much shorter lives than humans and their ageing is almost certainly something that will come all too soon. Few dogs remain as vigorous and youthful after ten, and the larger the dog, the faster and sooner the ageing process. The truth is that when we take on a pet the only certainty is that it will not end well. One of you – and probably the pet – is going to die relatively soon, and managing that death is a duty of care as important as any part of its life.

But it is hard. To have the clarity to decide that worthwhile life is over, unclouded by sentiment or just naked affection, takes more than most of us can muster. So we cling to a life measured by memory and overlook the humiliations of an ageing body, telling ourselves that caring for an old dog is a sign of our love and an act of responsibility.

But sometimes the kindest and most loving thing we can do for a dog is to humanely and painlessly end its life. I have always felt guilt over the two occasions when I postponed having a dog put down simply because I could not face the loss. In hindsight I let them suffer simply in order that I should not. It was the coward's way out.

When his time comes, Nigel will be buried in the coppice next to Beaufort, just along from Red, in the shade of the wild cherry that I planted in 1993. The roots will be hard to chop through by then, the ground compacted and dry. But he will always be here, his gentle presence shadowing me, real and vital, part of the living essence of the garden.

But hopefully that will be many years from now. Anyway, as I write this, Nigel has just deposited a ball on my lap – it's time for a walk.

Dramatis Caninae

MAADA

Yellow Labrador 1960–1972. First childhood family dog.

BENGY

Beagle 1964–1969. My mother's much-loved dog. An uncontrollable wanderer.

SAM

Black Labrador 1965–1977. Family dog that increasingly became my companion on long teenage angst-ridden walks.

GRETEL

Yellow Labrador 1976–1986. My twenty-first birthday present and my inseparable, loyal friend.

ERIC

Terrier (Jack Russell/fox terrier cross) 1982–1992. My mother's present to Sarah. Belligerent, bolshie and obsessed by bricks.

BAFFIN
Blackdog (Newfoundland/husky/Labrador cross) 1985–1988 (1994) Brother of Beaufort. Went to live on a Scottish island.

BEAUFORT
Blackdog 1985–1999. Brother of Baffin. Sensitive, fiercely loyal and a true one-man dog. Buried in coppice at Longmeadow.

POPPY
Jack Russell terrier 1992–2005. Daughter of Eric. Mild and meek until she came across rats or other dogs. Then her father's ferocious genes came to the fore. Buried in coppice at Longmeadow.

RED
Blackdog 1995–2006. Niece of Baffin and Beaufort. Huge, gentle and adored by all. Buried in coppice at Longmeadow.

NIGEL
Golden retriever. Born 17 May 2008. Our Hero. Getting hairier.

NELLIE
Golden retriever. Born 22 September 2015. Naughty. Very naughty.

Acknowledgements

Every book feels to its author like a private and often lonely journey although every book is always a collaborative process. But three people in particular have supported, influenced and guided me. Gillon Aitken's wise counsel and experience set me on the right road - and kept me to it. Lisa Highton at Two Roads steered the book through publication with an unflustered and gently supportive hand. Alexandra Henderson's endless enthusiasm, including many hours of practical help, nurtured this book from a hesitant notion, through false starts into the object you hold in your hands. To all three I am extremely grateful.

Last, but by no means least, I must thank my son Adam for his generosity to both myself and Nigel.

Permissions and Picture Credits

P100-101 – Extract from T H White's *The Sword in the Stone* reprinted by permission of HarperCollins Publishers Ltd and the T H White Estate. © T H White 1938

Integrated black and white pictures on pages i, ix, 6, 39, 93, 240, 263, 271 © Marsha Arnold. All other pictures are from the author's personal family collection.

Colour pictures in plate section p13 picture 2 and page 16 © Marsha Arnold. All other pictures are from the author's personal family collection.

Every reasonable effort has been made to contact the copyright holders, but if there are any errors or omissions Two Roads will be pleased to insert the appropriate acknowledgement in any subsequent printing of this publication.

Monty Don is the author of many best-selling books including *The Complete Gardener, The Ivington Diaries, Around The World in 80 Gardens, From Fork to Fork* and *The Jewel Garden*, written with his wife Sarah and also published by Two Roads. For the past 30 years he has written and presented many television programmes and since 2003 has been the lead presenter of *Gardeners' World*, ably assisted by Nigel, which is filmed in his garden in Herefordshire.

@TheMontyDon

The Jewel Garden is the story of the garden that over the past decade has bloomed from the muddy fields around the Dons' Tudor farmhouse, a perfect metaphor for Monty and Sarah's own rise from the ashes of a spectacular commercial failure.

At the same time *The Jewel Garden* is the story of a creative partnership that has weathered the greatest storm, and a testament to the healing powers of the soil.

Written in an optimistic, autobiographical vein, Monty and Sarah's story is truly an exploration of what it means to be a gardener.

Stories . . . voices . . . places . . . lives

We hope you enjoyed *Nigel*. If you'd like to know more about this book or any other title on our list, please go to www. tworoadsbooks.com

For news on forthcoming Two Roads titles, please sign up for our newsletter.

enquiries@tworoadsbooks.com

TwoRoadsBooks